The Complete Java Developer's Handbook

Master Java from the Ground Up, with Real-World Projects

Greyson Chesterfield

COPYRIGHT

DISCLAIMER

Introduction

In an age where new programming languages are continually emerging, it might seem surprising that Java, first released in 1995, remains as relevant and essential as ever. Yet, from mobile applications and enterprise systems to cloud-based solutions and even microservices, Java's robustness, flexibility, and reliability have stood the test of time. Whether you're developing the backend for a global e-commerce platform or creating a streamlined Android app, Java is likely to be part of your toolkit. It's no wonder that Java remains one of the most sought-after skills for developers, with countless businesses around the world relying on it every day.

Why Learn Java?

Java's ongoing popularity is no accident. It was designed from the beginning to be versatile, secure, and performance-oriented, all while being accessible to developers of varying skill levels. As one of the first languages to champion the "write once, run anywhere" philosophy, Java provides a robust platform that allows code to run on any device equipped with the Java Virtual Machine (JVM), whether it's a server, desktop, or mobile device. This cross-platform capability has made Java the go-to language for large, complex systems that require reliability and security over the long haul.

Beyond just functionality, Java's structure promotes good coding practices, making it an excellent language for beginners. It's object-oriented, which means it organizes data and functions in ways that closely mirror real-world objects, making it easier to conceptualize, manage, and extend code. With Java, you'll not only learn programming but also build the kind of mindset that professional developers use to solve complex problems every day.

Who This Book is For

"The Complete Java Developer's Handbook" is crafted for anyone eager to master Java from the ground up. It's perfect for beginners who want a strong foundation and a guide through their first programming projects. Intermediate programmers will find deeper dives into concepts that will strengthen their skills, such as multithreading, collections, and database connectivity. If you're a seasoned developer looking to refine your Java knowledge, this book can serve as a refresher and a source of inspiration, especially through the real-world projects.

In short, this book is for anyone who wants to learn Java practically and systematically, with the goal of building real-world applications that are relevant to today's development landscape.

What You'll Learn in This Book

This book covers Java comprehensively, from its basic syntax and foundational principles to more advanced concepts and industry best practices. Each chapter builds on the last, guiding you from Java's core language features to more specialized topics. You'll start with the basics—setting up your environment, understanding data types, control flows, and functions—then gradually progress to advanced areas like multithreading, design patterns, and database connectivity.

Each chapter includes a hands-on project, providing a practical application of the topics covered. These projects range from building simple console applications to creating full-fledged systems with user interfaces and backend connectivity. By the end of each project, you'll have a concrete example of how Java is used in real-world applications, reinforcing both the language syntax and the development concepts discussed.

Real-World Relevance

A primary goal of this book is to equip you with skills you can apply directly in a professional setting. Java developers are in high demand across many sectors—banking, e-commerce, healthcare, and more. By tackling projects that reflect real-world applications, you'll not only understand how Java works but also why it's used the way it is. You'll learn to think like a developer, focusing on scalability, maintainability, and best practices.

For example, in Chapter 3, you'll create a Library Management System that simulates borrowing and returning books. This project will introduce you to the core concepts of Object-Oriented Programming (OOP)—encapsulation, inheritance, and polymorphism—which are essential in modern software development. Later, when working with databases in Chapter 10, you'll build an Employee Management System that stores information in a structured, retrievable format, similar to how professional applications manage user data.

How This Book is Structured

This handbook is organized to take you through a progressive journey in Java:

- **Chapters 1-5** cover the fundamentals of Java: syntax, control flows, data types, and essential programming constructs. These foundational skills will prepare you for building more complex applications.

- **Chapters 6-8** delve into intermediate topics, such as file input/output, networking, and multithreading, which are crucial for creating responsive and data-driven applications.

- **Chapters 9-11** focus on user interfaces, database connectivity, and deployment. These chapters will guide you through creating applications with JavaFX for graphical interfaces and using JDBC for database operations.

- **Chapters 12-15** introduce advanced topics such as testing, design patterns, and frameworks. Here, you'll learn industry-standard techniques for improving code quality and structuring applications efficiently, culminating in an exploration of the powerful Spring Framework for building robust, scalable web applications.

How to Approach This Book

The best way to learn Java is to code—actively and consistently. Each chapter is designed with this in mind, encouraging you to experiment, build, and test as you go. As you read, I encourage you to dive into the projects at the end of each chapter. These aren't just exercises; they're practical applications of the skills you're learning, each project carefully selected to mimic real-world needs. Don't worry if you find yourself stuck; persistence and practice are your best friends in programming.

While the book can be read from start to finish, feel free to revisit earlier chapters or skip to topics of particular interest. Each chapter is designed to be self-contained, allowing you to focus on what matters most to your learning journey.

The Journey Ahead

Embarking on this journey might feel challenging at times, but remember: every seasoned developer was once a beginner, too. Java may have a learning curve, but with patience, persistence, and practical experience, you'll find yourself not only mastering the language but also building the kind of problem-solving mindset that is crucial in the tech industry.

This book isn't just about learning Java syntax or memorizing rules—it's about understanding the "why" behind the "what." By the time you finish, you'll have a solid grasp of Java fundamentals, be capable of building sophisticated applications, and be equipped with the skills to pursue further learning independently.

Java has empowered countless developers to create applications that shape our world. Whether you're here to start a new career, build a passion project, or simply challenge yourself, you're in the right place. Let's get started, and welcome to "The Complete Java Developer's Handbook"—your guide to mastering Java and becoming a capable, confident developer.

Chapter 1: Getting Started with Java Development

Introduction to Java

Java has established itself as one of the most popular programming languages in the world, used across a vast array of industries and application types—from web development to Android applications, enterprise systems, and even gaming. Its reliability and scalability have made Java a cornerstone of modern software development, and learning it provides a strong foundation for anyone entering the field.

In this chapter, we'll set up everything you need to start programming in Java, including installing the necessary tools, understanding Java's structure, and writing your first Java program. By the end, you'll have a functional Java development environment and a clear idea of how Java code is organized.

1.1 Understanding the Java Development Environment

What is the JDK (Java Development Kit)?

The JDK (Java Development Kit) is the primary software development kit for writing Java applications. It provides tools to compile, run, and debug Java code. Within the JDK, you'll find:

- **Java Compiler (javac)**: Converts Java source code (written in .java files) into bytecode (.class files).

- **Java Virtual Machine (JVM)**: Runs the compiled bytecode, making Java applications platform-independent by allowing the same code to run on any system with a JVM.

- **Libraries**: Pre-written code for standard Java functions, including data manipulation, I/O, and networking.

Java's "write once, run anywhere" capability is possible because of the JVM, which allows code written on one operating system to run on another without modification. For this reason, setting up the JDK is essential to start programming in Java.

Downloading and Installing the JDK

1. **Download the JDK**: Visit the official Oracle website to download the latest version of the JDK (or choose an open-source distribution like OpenJDK).

2. **Install the JDK**: Follow the installation instructions specific to your operating system. The installer will guide you through the process, ensuring the JDK is correctly configured.

3. **Set the PATH Environment Variable**: After installation, add the bin directory of the JDK to your system's PATH environment variable. This allows you to run Java commands like javac and java from any command line location.

Setting Up an IDE (Integrated Development Environment)

While you could write and compile Java code using a simple text editor, an IDE significantly enhances productivity by providing helpful features like code completion, debugging, and error checking. Three popular IDEs for Java development are:

- **IntelliJ IDEA**: Known for its robust features, IntelliJ IDEA is widely used in the industry. It provides extensive support for Java projects and integrates well with libraries and frameworks.

- **Eclipse**: A long-standing favorite among Java developers, Eclipse is open-source and highly customizable.

- **NetBeans**: An Oracle-supported IDE that's also open-source, particularly useful for beginners due to its simpler interface and integration with JavaFX.

For this book, we'll use IntelliJ IDEA for its ease of use and versatility. However, the instructions provided can be adapted for other IDEs.

1.2 Writing Your First Java Program

With your environment set up, it's time to write a simple Java program. Let's start with the classic "Hello, World!" program, which will introduce you to Java's basic structure.

Creating a New Java Project

1. **Open IntelliJ IDEA** and select "New Project."

2. Choose "Java" and then select the JDK you installed earlier.

3. Name your project "HelloJava" and click "Finish."

You now have a blank Java project. Projects in Java are structured into packages and classes, and we'll start with a single class to keep things simple.

Understanding Java's Basic Structure

Every Java application consists of classes and methods. A Java class is a blueprint for creating objects and methods, which are blocks of code that perform specific tasks. In Java, every application must have a class that contains a main method, which serves as the entry point for the application.

Writing the Code

1. **Create a Class**:

   o Right-click on the src directory in your project and select "New" > "Java Class."

   o Name the class HelloWorld and click "OK."

2. **Add the main Method**:

   o Inside the HelloWorld class, type the following code:

java

public class HelloWorld {

```java
    public static void main(String[] args) {

        System.out.println("Hello, World!");

    }

}
```

Let's break down what each part of this code does:

- public class HelloWorld: Declares a class named HelloWorld. The public keyword means it's accessible from outside the class.

- public static void main(String[] args): This line declares the main method, which is where the program starts execution. The parameters (String[] args) allow the program to accept command-line arguments.

- System.out.println("Hello, World!");: This line outputs text to the console. In this case, it prints "Hello, World!"

Running the Program

To run your program, right-click on HelloWorld.java and select "Run 'HelloWorld.main()'." You should see the text "Hello, World!" displayed in the console. Congratulations! You've just written and executed your first Java program.

1.3 Java Basics: Syntax, Data Types, and Variables

Now that we've run a simple program, let's dive into some of Java's foundational elements. This section covers essential syntax rules, data types, and variable declaration.

Basic Syntax

Java syntax might look a bit daunting at first, but it follows a logical structure. Here are some key points:

- **Case Sensitivity**: Java is case-sensitive, so HelloWorld and helloworld would be treated as different classes.

- **Class Naming**: By convention, Java class names should start with a capital letter (e.g., MyClass).

- **Braces {}**: Curly braces are used to define blocks of code, such as the start and end of classes and methods.

- **Semicolons ;**: Every statement in Java ends with a semicolon.

Data Types and Variables

Java is a strongly typed language, meaning every variable must have a data type. Here's a quick overview of common data types:

- **Primitive Data Types**:

- int: Integer values, e.g., int age = 25;

- double: Floating-point numbers, e.g., double price = 9.99;

- char: Single characters, e.g., char grade = 'A';

- boolean: True or false values, e.g., boolean isJavaFun = true;

- **Non-Primitive Data Types**: These include arrays, strings, and objects created from classes. For example:

  - String name = "John Doe";

To declare and initialize a variable, specify its type, name, and value:

java

int year = 2022;

String welcomeMessage = "Welcome to Java!";

1.4 Control Flow Statements

Control flow statements manage the order of execution in a program, which includes conditional statements and loops.

Conditional Statements

Java provides conditional statements like if, else if, and else to make decisions based on conditions:

java

```java
int age = 20;
if (age >= 18) {
    System.out.println("You are an adult.");
} else {
    System.out.println("You are not an adult.");
}
```

Loops

Loops let you execute code repeatedly. Two common loop types in Java are for and while:

- **For Loop**: Used when the number of iterations is known.

java

```java
for (int i = 0; i < 5; i++) {
    System.out.println("Iteration: " + i);
}
```

- **While Loop**: Runs as long as a specified condition is true.

java

```java
int count = 0;
while (count < 5) {
    System.out.println("Count: " + count);
    count++;
}
```

1.5 Basic Console Project: User Greeting

With these basics, let's create a simple project that combines input, variables, and output to greet the user.

Project Steps

1. **Create a New Java Class**: Name it UserGreeting.

2. **Write Code to Take User Input**:

   o Use the Scanner class to accept input from the console.

java

```java
import java.util.Scanner;

public class UserGreeting {
    public static void main(String[] args) {
        Scanner scanner = new Scanner(System.in);

        System.out.print("Enter your name: ");
        String name = scanner.nextLine();

        System.out.println("Hello, " + name + "! Welcome to Java.");

        scanner.close();
    }
}
```

Explanation:

- Scanner scanner = new Scanner(System.in);:
  Creates a Scanner object to read input from the
  console.

- String name = scanner.nextLine();: Reads a line
  of text input by the user.

- System.out.println("Hello, " + name + "!");:
  Displays a personalized greeting.

Run the UserGreeting program, enter your name, and
see your greeting printed on the console.

Conclusion

In this chapter, you've successfully set up your Java
development environment, written your first Java
program, and learned about Java's basic syntax,
variables, and control flow. You also completed a
simple project that takes user input and displays a
custom greeting, demonstrating how quickly you can
create interactive programs with Java.

This foundation will support everything we cover in
the coming chapters, from object-oriented
programming to database connectivity and beyond.
With each step, your understanding of Java will
deepen, building up your skills until you're ready to
tackle advanced projects. Let's continue to Chapter 2,
where you'll explore Java's syntax and data handling
more thoroughly!

Chapter 2: Core Java Syntax and Basics

Introduction to Core Java Syntax

Java's syntax might seem complex at first, but once you break it down, it follows a logical and consistent pattern. Each part of Java's syntax serves a purpose in creating clear, organized code. In this chapter, we'll look at the core elements that make up the Java language, focusing on writing efficient, readable code.

2.1 Variables and Data Types

What are Variables?

Variables are containers that store data values. In Java, each variable must have a specific type, which determines what kind of data it can hold. There are two primary types of data in Java: **primitive data types** and **reference data types**.

Primitive Data Types

Java has eight built-in primitive data types:

- **byte**: 1-byte integer, ranging from -128 to 127.
- **short**: 2-byte integer, from -32,768 to 32,767.
- **int**: 4-byte integer, commonly used for numeric values.
- **long**: 8-byte integer, suitable for large numeric values.
- **float**: 4-byte floating-point number, used for single-precision decimals.
- **double**: 8-byte floating-point number, for double-precision decimals.
- **char**: 2-byte character, stores a single character.
- **boolean**: Stores either true or false.

Example of variable declarations:

java

```
int age = 25;

double price = 19.99;

char grade = 'A';

boolean isAvailable = true;
```

Reference Data Types

Reference data types store references to objects, rather than raw data. The most common reference type is **String**, which holds sequences of characters.

java

```java
String name = "Java Developer";
```

Type Casting

Type casting is converting one data type into another. There are two types of casting:

1. **Implicit Casting**: Java automatically converts smaller types to larger types (e.g., int to double).

2. **Explicit Casting**: Manually converting larger types to smaller types (e.g., double to int), which may lose precision.

Example of explicit casting:

java

```java
double price = 19.99;

int roundedPrice = (int) price; // Now roundedPrice holds 19
```

2.2 Operators in Java

Operators perform operations on variables and values. Java has several types of operators:

Arithmetic Operators

These perform basic arithmetic operations:

- + (addition)
- - (subtraction)
- * (multiplication)
- / (division)
- % (modulus, gives remainder)

Example:

java

```
int a = 10;
int b = 3;
int sum = a + b; // sum is 13
int remainder = a % b; // remainder is 1
```

Assignment Operators

These assign values to variables:

- = (simple assignment)
- +=, -=, *=, /= (compound assignment)

Example:

java

int count = 5;

count += 3; // Now count is 8

Comparison Operators

These compare two values and return a boolean result:

- == (equal to)
- != (not equal to)
- <, >, <=, >=

Example:

java

int x = 10;

int y = 5;

boolean isEqual = (x == y); // isEqual is false

Logical Operators

These perform logical operations and return a boolean result:

- && (logical AND)
- || (logical OR)

- ! (logical NOT)

Example:

java

```
boolean isAdult = true;

boolean hasLicense = false;

boolean canDrive = isAdult && hasLicense; // canDrive is false
```

2.3 Control Flow Statements

Control flow statements manage the order of execution in a program and are essential for decision-making and looping.

Conditional Statements

Conditional statements allow programs to make decisions based on conditions.

If-Else Statements

The if-else statement executes code based on a condition.

java

```java
int age = 18;
if (age >= 18) {
    System.out.println("You are an adult.");
} else {
    System.out.println("You are not an adult.");
}
```

Switch Statements

Switch statements provide a way to execute code based on the value of a variable, often used for multiple choices.

java

```java
int day = 3;
switch (day) {
    case 1:
        System.out.println("Monday");
        break;
    case 2:
        System.out.println("Tuesday");
        break;
    case 3:
```

```java
        System.out.println("Wednesday");
        break;
    default:
        System.out.println("Other day");
}
```

Looping Statements

Loops allow you to repeat a block of code multiple times.

For Loop

The for loop repeats code a specific number of times.

java

```java
for (int i = 0; i < 5; i++) {
    System.out.println("Iteration: " + i);
}
```

While Loop

The while loop repeats code as long as a condition is true.

java

```java
int i = 0;
```

```java
while (i < 5) {
    System.out.println("Count: " + i);
    i++;
}
```

Do-While Loop

The do-while loop is similar to while but guarantees at least one execution.

java

```java
int j = 0;
do {
    System.out.println("Count: " + j);
    j++;
} while (j < 5);
```

2.4 Arrays

Arrays are a way to store multiple values of the same type in a single variable.

Declaring and Initializing Arrays

java

```java
int[] numbers = {1, 2, 3, 4, 5}; // Array of integers
```

```java
String[] names = {"Alice", "Bob", "Charlie"}; // Array of strings
```

Accessing Array Elements

Array elements are accessed using their index (starting at 0).

java

```java
System.out.println(numbers[2]); // Outputs 3
```

Looping Through Arrays

java

```java
for (int i = 0; i < numbers.length; i++) {
    System.out.println(numbers[i]);
}
```

Alternatively, use the enhanced for-loop:

java

```java
for (int num : numbers) {
    System.out.println(num);
```

}

2.5 Basic Project: Simple Calculator

Now that we have the basics, let's apply them in a small project: building a simple calculator. This calculator will take two numbers and an operation as input and display the result.

Project Steps

1. **Set up the Class and Scanner**

java

```java
import java.util.Scanner;

public class SimpleCalculator {
    public static void main(String[] args) {
        Scanner scanner = new Scanner(System.in);

        System.out.print("Enter first number: ");
        double num1 = scanner.nextDouble();

        System.out.print("Enter an operator (+, -, *, /): ");
```

```java
char operator = scanner.next().charAt(0);

System.out.print("Enter second number: ");
double num2 = scanner.nextDouble();

double result;

switch (operator) {
    case '+':
        result = num1 + num2;
        break;
    case '-':
        result = num1 - num2;
        break;
    case '*':
        result = num1 * num2;
        break;
    case '/':
        if (num2 != 0) {
            result = num1 / num2;
        } else {
```

```java
                System.out.println("Cannot divide by
zero.");

                scanner.close();

                return;

            }
            break;
        default:
            System.out.println("Invalid operator");
            scanner.close();
            return;
    }


    System.out.println("The result is: " + result);
    scanner.close();

    }
}
```

Explanation

- **Getting Input**: The program uses a Scanner to receive user input for two numbers and an operator.

- **Switch Statement**: The switch handles each operator, performing the chosen operation.

- **Error Handling**: Checks for division by zero, printing an error message if detected.

Run this program and try entering different values and operators to see the results.

Conclusion

In this chapter, you learned about Java's core syntax, including data types, variables, operators, and control flow statements. You also saw how to use arrays to store and manipulate multiple values and created a simple calculator program, applying these foundational concepts in a practical way.

Mastering these basics is essential, as they form the foundation for everything else you'll learn in Java. In the next chapter, we'll explore Object-Oriented Programming, diving into how to design programs around objects and classes, which are key components of Java's approach to software development.

Chapter 3: Object-Oriented Programming in Java

Introduction to Object-Oriented Programming (OOP)

Object-Oriented Programming is based on the idea of creating objects, which are instances of classes that encapsulate data and methods. This approach makes code more modular, readable, and reusable, allowing developers to tackle complex projects with ease. In Java, everything revolves around objects and classes, making it an ideal language for learning and implementing OOP.

Java's support for OOP enables developers to create applications that are modular and easy to expand. By understanding the fundamentals of OOP in Java, you can create systems that mirror real-world structures, which is one of the reasons Java is so widely used in enterprise-level applications.

3.1 Understanding Classes and Objects

What is a Class?

A class is a blueprint for creating objects. It defines the properties (attributes) and behaviors (methods) that an object of that class will have. For example, a Car class might define properties such as make, model, and year, along with behaviors like start() and stop().

java

```java
public class Car {
    // Attributes (properties)
    String make;
    String model;
    int year;

    // Constructor
    public Car(String make, String model, int year) {
        this.make = make;
        this.model = model;
```

```java
        this.year = year;
    }


    // Methods (behaviors)
    public void start() {
        System.out.println("The car has started.");
    }


    public void stop() {
        System.out.println("The car has stopped.");
    }
}
```

What is an Object?

An object is an instance of a class. In our example, you might create an object of Car like this:

java


```java
Car myCar = new Car("Toyota", "Corolla", 2020);
```

This myCar object now has its own make, model, and year attributes, and can perform actions defined in the Car class, such as start() and stop().

3.2 Encapsulation

Encapsulation is the concept of bundling data (attributes) and methods (behaviors) within a class and restricting direct access to them from outside the class. This is achieved by marking attributes as private and providing public getter and setter methods to control access.

Example of Encapsulation

java

```java
public class BankAccount {
    private double balance; // Private attribute

    // Constructor
    public BankAccount(double initialBalance) {
        balance = initialBalance;
    }

    // Getter method for balance
    public double getBalance() {
        return balance;
    }
```

```java
    // Setter method for depositing money

    public void deposit(double amount) {

        if (amount > 0) {

            balance += amount;

        }

    }


    // Setter method for withdrawing money

    public void withdraw(double amount) {

        if (amount > 0 && amount <= balance) {

            balance -= amount;

        }

    }

}
```

In this example, the balance attribute is private, meaning it can only be accessed and modified through the getBalance(), deposit(), and withdraw() methods. This protects the data within the object, ensuring that any changes are controlled and consistent.

3.3 Inheritance

Inheritance allows a class to inherit attributes and methods from another class, promoting code reusability and creating a hierarchy. In Java, inheritance is achieved using the extends keyword.

Example of Inheritance

Suppose we have a Vehicle class, and we want to create a Car class that inherits from it.

java

```java
public class Vehicle {
    String type;

    public void start() {
        System.out.println("Vehicle started.");
    }
}


public class Car extends Vehicle {
    String make;
    String model;
```

```java
    public Car(String make, String model) {

        this.type = "Car";

        this.make = make;

        this.model = model;

    }


    public void showDetails() {

        System.out.println("Type: " + type + ", Make: " +
make + ", Model: " + model);

    }
}
```

In this example, Car inherits from Vehicle, meaning it automatically has access to the type attribute and the start() method. The Car class can add its own properties and methods as well, providing additional details like make and model.

The super Keyword

The super keyword allows a subclass to refer to its superclass, often used to call the superclass's constructor or methods.

java

```java
public Car(String make, String model) {
```

```java
super(); // Calls the Vehicle constructor
this.make = make;
this.model = model;
}
```

3.4 Polymorphism

Polymorphism allows objects to take on multiple forms. In Java, it primarily manifests in two ways: **method overriding** and **method overloading**.

Method Overloading

Method overloading occurs when multiple methods in the same class have the same name but different parameters.

java

```java
public class Printer {
    public void print(String text) {
        System.out.println(text);
    }
```

```java
    public void print(int number) {

        System.out.println(number);

    }

}
```

Here, both print methods have the same name but accept different types of arguments. Java automatically determines which method to call based on the parameter types provided.

Method Overriding

Method overriding occurs when a subclass redefines a method from its superclass. This allows the subclass to provide its own implementation.

java

```java
public class Animal {

    public void sound() {

        System.out.println("Animal makes a sound");

    }

}


public class Dog extends Animal {
```

```java
@Override

public void sound() {

    System.out.println("Dog barks");

}

}
```

In this example, Dog overrides the sound() method from Animal, providing a specialized version.

Dynamic Binding

Polymorphism is particularly powerful when combined with **dynamic binding**, which allows Java to decide which method to execute at runtime based on the actual object type.

java

```java
Animal myAnimal = new Dog();

myAnimal.sound(); // Outputs "Dog barks" because the actual object is of type Dog
```

3.5 Abstraction

Abstraction focuses on showing only the essential features of an object and hiding the unnecessary details. In Java, abstraction is achieved using **abstract classes** and **interfaces**.

Abstract Classes

An abstract class is a class that cannot be instantiated. It often contains one or more abstract methods—methods declared without an implementation.

java

```java
public abstract class Shape {
    abstract void draw(); // Abstract method

    public void display() {
        System.out.println("Displaying a shape.");
    }
}


public class Circle extends Shape {
    @Override
    public void draw() {
        System.out.println("Drawing a circle.");
    }
}
```

In this example, Shape is an abstract class with an abstract method draw(). Any subclass of Shape must implement draw().

Interfaces

An interface is a contract that a class can implement, defining methods that the class must implement.

java

```java
public interface Movable {
    void move();
}


public class Vehicle implements Movable {
    @Override
    public void move() {
        System.out.println("Vehicle is moving.");
    }
}
```

In Java, a class can implement multiple interfaces, allowing for more flexible code design.

3.6 Project: Library Management System

To apply these OOP principles, let's create a basic Library Management System that uses classes, inheritance, encapsulation, and polymorphism.

Project Structure

1. **Base Class (Book)**: Create a Book class to represent a book with attributes for the title, author, and ISBN.

2. **Subclass (EBook)**: Create an EBook subclass that extends Book with additional attributes like file size and format.

3. **Library Class**: Manage a collection of Book and EBook objects, using polymorphism to treat them uniformly.

4. **User Interaction**: Allow users to view details of available books and add new books to the collection.

Code Implementation

1. **Define the Book Class**

java

```java
public class Book {
    private String title;
```

```java
    private String author;

    private String ISBN;


    public Book(String title, String author, String ISBN)
{
        this.title = title;

        this.author = author;

        this.ISBN = ISBN;

    }


    public String getTitle() {
        return title;

    }


    public void displayInfo() {
        System.out.println("Title: " + title + ", Author: " +
author + ", ISBN: " + ISBN);

    }
}
```

2. **Create the EBook Subclass**

java

```java
public class EBook extends Book {
    private double fileSize;

    public EBook(String title, String author, String ISBN, double fileSize) {
        super(title, author, ISBN);
        this.fileSize = fileSize;
    }

    @Override
    public void displayInfo() {
        super.displayInfo();
        System.out.println("File Size: " + fileSize + " MB");
    }
}
```

3. **Library Class to Manage Books**

java

```java
import java.util.ArrayList;
```

```java
public class Library {

    private ArrayList<Book> books = new
ArrayList<>();

    public void addBook(Book book) {
        books.add(book);
    }

    public void displayBooks() {
        for (Book book : books) {
            book.displayInfo();
            System.out.println("-----");
        }
    }
}
```

4. User Interaction in Main Class

java

```java
public class Main {
    public static void main(String[] args) {
```

```java
        Library library = new Library();


        Book book1 = new Book("Java Programming",
"Author A", "123456789");

        EBook ebook1 = new EBook("Advanced Java",
"Author B", "987654321", 5.6);


        library.addBook(book1);

        library.addBook(ebook1);


        library.displayBooks();
    }

}
```

Explanation

- The Book class represents basic books, while EBook inherits from Book and adds specific properties.

- Library holds a collection of Book objects, demonstrating polymorphism by treating Book and EBook objects similarly.

- The Main class allows the user to add and view books, illustrating how OOP principles work in a real-world context.

Conclusion

In this chapter, you learned the fundamental principles of OOP—encapsulation, inheritance, polymorphism, and abstraction—and how to implement them in Java. We applied these concepts in a Library Management System project, showing how OOP can structure and simplify real-world applications. With this foundation, you're ready to move on to more advanced Java concepts, where you'll build on these principles to create more complex and powerful applications.

In the next chapter, we'll explore Java's Collections Framework, a set of data structures and utilities for efficiently storing and managing data.

Chapter 4: Java Collections Framework

Introduction to the Java Collections Framework

The Java Collections Framework is a library that provides data structures and algorithms to manage groups of objects. Instead of writing custom implementations for common structures like lists, sets, and maps, the framework offers ready-to-use, highly optimized implementations. Java collections can store almost any kind of data, allowing you to focus on solving complex problems without having to worry about the underlying details of data storage and retrieval.

4.1 Core Interfaces of the Collections Framework

The Java Collections Framework is built around a set of core interfaces. Each interface defines a type of collection with specific behaviors, allowing developers to choose the best type for their needs. Here are the four main interfaces in the framework:

- **List**: An ordered collection (also known as a sequence) that allows duplicate elements.

- **Set**: A collection that does not allow duplicate elements.

- **Queue**: A collection used to hold elements prior to processing, following a specific order.

- **Map**: A collection of key-value pairs, where each key is unique.

Each of these interfaces has specific characteristics and use cases, which we'll cover in the following sections.

4.2 The List Interface

The List interface represents an ordered collection of elements, allowing duplicates and maintaining the order in which elements are inserted. Lists are ideal when you need to access elements by their position or maintain the insertion order.

ArrayList

An ArrayList is a resizable array implementation of the List interface. It provides fast random access to elements but can be slower when adding or removing elements in the middle of the list due to shifting.

java

```java
import java.util.ArrayList;

public class ListExample {
    public static void main(String[] args) {
        ArrayList<String> names = new ArrayList<>();
        names.add("Alice");
        names.add("Bob");
        names.add("Charlie");

        System.out.println(names.get(1)); // Output: Bob
    }
}
```

LinkedList

LinkedList is a doubly-linked list implementation of the List interface. It performs better than ArrayList for insertions and deletions at the beginning or middle of the list but is slower for random access.

java

```java
import java.util.LinkedList;

public class LinkedListExample {
    public static void main(String[] args) {
        LinkedList<String> queue = new LinkedList<>();
        queue.add("First");
        queue.add("Second");
        queue.addFirst("New First");

        System.out.println(queue.get(0)); // Output: New First
    }
}
```

When to Use List

- Use ArrayList when you need fast access to elements by index.

- Use LinkedList when your application requires frequent insertions or deletions in the list.

4.3 The Set Interface

The Set interface represents a collection of unique elements. Sets do not allow duplicate elements, which makes them suitable for cases where uniqueness is required.

HashSet

HashSet is an implementation of the Set interface that uses a hash table to store elements. It provides constant-time performance for basic operations like adding and checking for the presence of elements, but it does not guarantee order.

java

```
import java.util.HashSet;


public class HashSetExample {
    public static void main(String[] args) {
        HashSet<String> set = new HashSet<>();
        set.add("Apple");
        set.add("Banana");
        set.add("Apple"); // Duplicate, won't be added
```

```
    System.out.println(set); // Output: [Banana,
Apple]

    }

}
```

LinkedHashSet

LinkedHashSet is similar to HashSet but maintains the insertion order of elements. It's useful when you want both uniqueness and order.

java

```java
import java.util.LinkedHashSet;


public class LinkedHashSetExample {
    public static void main(String[] args) {
        LinkedHashSet<String> orderedSet = new
LinkedHashSet<>();

        orderedSet.add("First");

        orderedSet.add("Second");

        orderedSet.add("First"); // Duplicate, won't be
added


        System.out.println(orderedSet); // Output: [First,
Second]
```

        }

}

TreeSet

TreeSet is a sorted set based on a tree structure (usually a Red-Black tree). Elements are stored in ascending order, making it ideal when a sorted set is required.

java

```
import java.util.TreeSet;

public class TreeSetExample {
    public static void main(String[] args) {
        TreeSet<Integer> numbers = new TreeSet<>();
        numbers.add(20);
        numbers.add(5);
        numbers.add(10);

        System.out.println(numbers); // Output: [5, 10, 20]
    }
}
```

4.4 The Queue Interface

The Queue interface represents a collection designed for holding elements prior to processing. Queues typically follow a FIFO (First-In, First-Out) order.

PriorityQueue

PriorityQueue is a queue that orders elements based on their natural ordering or by a comparator provided at the time of creation. It's commonly used for tasks where elements are processed by priority.

java

```java
import java.util.PriorityQueue;

public class PriorityQueueExample {
    public static void main(String[] args) {
        PriorityQueue<Integer> queue = new PriorityQueue<>();
        queue.add(30);
        queue.add(20);
        queue.add(10);
```

```java
        System.out.println(queue.poll()); // Output: 10
(lowest priority)
    }

}
```

LinkedList as Queue

The LinkedList class also implements the Queue interface, offering an easy way to use a linked list structure for FIFO operations.

java

```java
import java.util.LinkedList;

import java.util.Queue;


public class QueueExample {

    public static void main(String[] args) {

        Queue<String> queue = new LinkedList<>();

        queue.add("First");

        queue.add("Second");


        System.out.println(queue.poll()); // Output: First

    }
```

```
}
```

4.5 The Map Interface

The Map interface represents a collection of key-value pairs, where each key is unique. Maps are ideal when you need to associate values with keys.

HashMap

HashMap is an implementation of the Map interface that stores keys and values in a hash table. It allows null values and keys, but does not maintain order.

java

```java
import java.util.HashMap;


public class HashMapExample {
    public static void main(String[] args) {
        HashMap<String, Integer> map = new
HashMap<>();
        map.put("Alice", 30);
        map.put("Bob", 25);
```

```java
        System.out.println(map.get("Alice")); // Output:
30
    }
}
```

LinkedHashMap

LinkedHashMap is similar to HashMap but maintains the insertion order of elements, making it useful when order matters.

java

```java
import java.util.LinkedHashMap;


public class LinkedHashMapExample {
    public static void main(String[] args) {
        LinkedHashMap<String, Integer> orderedMap =
new LinkedHashMap<>();
        orderedMap.put("First", 1);
        orderedMap.put("Second", 2);


        System.out.println(orderedMap); // Output:
{First=1, Second=2}
    }
```

}

TreeMap

TreeMap is a sorted map implementation based on a Red-Black tree. It stores keys in ascending order, making it suitable for ordered data.

java

```java
import java.util.TreeMap;

public class TreeMapExample {
    public static void main(String[] args) {
        TreeMap<Integer, String> sortedMap = new TreeMap<>();
        sortedMap.put(3, "Three");
        sortedMap.put(1, "One");

        System.out.println(sortedMap); // Output: {1=One, 3=Three}
    }
}
```

4.6 Project: Student Record Management System

Let's apply the Java Collections Framework to build a basic Student Record Management System. This system will use a HashMap to store and retrieve student records based on unique student IDs.

Project Requirements

1. **Store student information**: Each student has an ID, name, and age.

2. **Add new students**: Users can add a new student record.

3. **View all students**: Display all student records.

4. **Search for a student by ID**: Retrieve a student's information using their ID.

Implementation

1. **Create the Student Class**

java

```
public class Student {
    private String id;
    private String name;
    private int age;
```

```java
public Student(String id, String name, int age) {
    this.id = id;
    this.name = name;
    this.age = age;
}

public String getId() {
    return id;
}

public String getName() {
    return name;
}

public int getAge() {
    return age;
}

@Override
public String toString() {
```

```java
        return "ID: " + id + ", Name: " + name + ", Age: " + age;
    }
}
```

2. Create the StudentManager Class

java

```java
import java.util.HashMap;
import java.util.Map;

public class StudentManager {
    private Map<String, Student> studentRecords = new HashMap<>();

    public void addStudent(Student student) {
        studentRecords.put(student.getId(), student);
    }

    public void viewAllStudents() {
        for (Student student : studentRecords.values()) {
            System.out.println(student);
```

```
        }
    }
```

```java
    public Student searchStudentById(String id) {
        return studentRecords.get(id);
    }
}
```

3. Main Class for User Interaction

java

```java
import java.util.Scanner;

public class Main {
    public static void main(String[] args) {
        StudentManager manager = new StudentManager();
        Scanner scanner = new Scanner(System.in);

        // Adding sample students
        manager.addStudent(new Student("S001", "Alice", 20));
```

```java
        manager.addStudent(new Student("S002", "Bob",
22));

        // Viewing all students
        System.out.println("All students:");
        manager.viewAllStudents();

        // Searching for a student by ID
        System.out.print("\nEnter student ID to search: ");
        String id = scanner.nextLine();
        Student student =
manager.searchStudentById(id);

        if (student != null) {
            System.out.println("Student found: " +
student);
        } else {
            System.out.println("Student not found.");
        }

        scanner.close();
    }
```

}

Explanation

- The Student class represents individual student records.

- The StudentManager class stores student records in a HashMap, allowing fast access by ID.

- The Main class provides basic interaction, allowing users to view all students and search by ID.

Conclusion

In this chapter, you learned about Java's Collections Framework, exploring different interfaces and their implementations, including List, Set, Queue, and Map. We applied this knowledge in a Student Record Management System, demonstrating how collections can simplify data management and retrieval.

In the next chapter, we'll dive into exception handling, exploring how to manage errors effectively in Java and build more resilient applications.

Chapter 5: Exception Handling and Debugging Techniques

Introduction to Exception Handling

In Java, an exception is an unexpected event that occurs during the execution of a program, disrupting its normal flow. Exceptions can occur due to user input errors, file I/O problems, or issues in the code itself. Java's exception handling mechanism provides a structured way to catch these events, handle them gracefully, and keep programs from crashing.

Java's approach to exception handling is centered around four key components:

1. **try**: Block of code where exceptions may occur.

2. **catch**: Handles the exception if one occurs.

3. **finally**: Executes code regardless of whether an exception occurred.

4. **throw/throws**: Used to explicitly throw an exception or declare it.

5.1 Types of Exceptions

Java exceptions fall into three main categories:

1. **Checked Exceptions**: These are exceptions that must be either handled in the code or declared in the method signature with throws. They usually result from external conditions outside the program's control, such as file I/O issues or network problems.

    o   Examples: IOException, SQLException

2. **Unchecked Exceptions**: Also known as runtime exceptions, these result from programming errors like logic mistakes or incorrect use of API methods. They are not checked at compile-time and can be avoided by careful programming.

    o   Examples: NullPointerException, ArrayIndexOutOfBoundsException, ArithmeticException

3. **Errors**: Errors are serious issues that applications generally should not try to handle,

such as out-of-memory errors. They are part of Java's error hierarchy but are not exceptions.

- o Examples: OutOfMemoryError, StackOverflowError

5.2 Exception Handling Syntax: try, catch, finally

The basic syntax for exception handling in Java involves the try, catch, and finally blocks. Let's examine each of these components.

Using try and catch Blocks

A try block contains code that may throw an exception. If an exception occurs, it's caught by a matching catch block, where you can handle it appropriately.

java

```java
public class ExceptionExample {
    public static void main(String[] args) {
        try {
            int result = 10 / 0; // Will cause
ArithmeticException
        } catch (ArithmeticException e) {
```

```java
            System.out.println("Cannot divide by zero!");
        }
    }
}
```

In this example, dividing by zero throws an ArithmeticException, which is then caught by the catch block. The program prints an error message and continues running, instead of crashing.

The finally Block

The finally block always executes after try and catch, regardless of whether an exception occurred. It's commonly used for cleanup operations, like closing file streams or releasing resources.

java

```java
import java.io.FileInputStream;

import java.io.IOException;


public class FinallyExample {
    public static void main(String[] args) {
        FileInputStream file = null;
        try {
            file = new FileInputStream("example.txt");
```

```java
        // Perform file operations
    } catch (IOException e) {
        System.out.println("File not found or I/O error.");
    } finally {
        try {
            if (file != null) file.close();
            System.out.println("File closed.");
        } catch (IOException e) {
            System.out.println("Failed to close the file.");
        }
    }
}
```

In this example, the finally block ensures that the file is closed even if an exception occurs during file operations.

5.3 Throwing and Declaring Exceptions

The throw Statement

The throw statement is used to explicitly throw an exception. This is useful when you want to indicate an error condition based on custom logic.

java

```java
public class ThrowExample {
    public static void main(String[] args) {
        try {
            checkAge(15);
        } catch (Exception e) {
            System.out.println(e.getMessage());
        }
    }


    public static void checkAge(int age) {
        if (age < 18) {
            throw new IllegalArgumentException("Age must be 18 or older.");
```

```
        }
    }
}
```

Here, if the age is below 18, the method throws an IllegalArgumentException with a custom message. This helps enforce specific business logic in your application.

The throws Keyword

The throws keyword is used in method declarations to indicate that the method may throw specific exceptions. This is typically done for checked exceptions.

java

```java
import java.io.FileNotFoundException;
import java.io.FileReader;

public class ThrowsExample {
    public static void main(String[] args) {
        try {
            readFile();
        } catch (FileNotFoundException e) {
            System.out.println("File not found.");
```

```java
    }
  }


  public static void readFile() throws
FileNotFoundException {

    FileReader file = new FileReader("example.txt");

    // Perform file reading operations

  }
}
```

The readFile() method declares that it may throw a FileNotFoundException. This informs any code calling readFile() that it must handle or propagate the exception.

5.4 Custom Exceptions

Java allows you to create custom exceptions by extending the Exception class (for checked exceptions) or the RuntimeException class (for unchecked exceptions). Custom exceptions are helpful when you want to create meaningful errors specific to your application's logic.

java

```java
public class InsufficientBalanceException extends
Exception {

    public InsufficientBalanceException(String
message) {

        super(message);

    }

}


public class BankAccount {

    private double balance;


    public void withdraw(double amount) throws
InsufficientBalanceException {

        if (amount > balance) {

            throw new
InsufficientBalanceException("Insufficient balance for
withdrawal.");

        }

        balance -= amount;

    }

}
```

In this example, InsufficientBalanceException is a custom exception that's thrown if the withdrawal amount exceeds the account balance, providing a clear, descriptive error for the user.

5.5 Common Debugging Techniques

Exception handling helps prevent crashes, but debugging techniques allow you to identify and fix problems in your code before they occur. Java IDEs like IntelliJ IDEA and Eclipse provide built-in debugging tools that can help you track down issues in your code.

Using Print Statements

A simple but effective debugging method is to print variable values and checkpoints to the console. Although limited, this method can quickly provide insights into variable states and code flow.

java

```
public class DebugExample {
    public static void main(String[] args) {
        int a = 5;
        int b = 0;
        System.out.println("a = " + a);
        System.out.println("b = " + b);
```

```
    int result = a / b; // This line will cause an
exception

    }

}
```

Setting Breakpoints

A more sophisticated approach to debugging involves using breakpoints. Breakpoints pause the program at specific lines, allowing you to examine the program state (variables, expressions, etc.) at that point.

1. **Set a Breakpoint**: In your IDE, click next to the line number where you want the program to pause.

2. **Run in Debug Mode**: Start the program in debug mode, and it will stop at the breakpoint.

3. **Inspect Variables**: Check the values of variables and step through code to understand how data flows.

Step Over, Step Into, and Step Out

When debugging, three useful commands help you control execution:

*   **Step Over**: Executes the next line of code, stepping over any function calls.

*   **Step Into**: Steps into a function call, allowing you to debug the function's code.

- **Step Out**: Completes the current function and returns to the caller, useful for exiting functions quickly.

Watch Expressions

Most IDEs allow you to set watch expressions, which let you monitor specific variables or expressions continuously during the debug session. This can help you see how values change over time.

5.6 Project: Bank Account Management with Exception Handling

In this project, we'll implement a BankAccount class that handles exceptions gracefully. Users can deposit and withdraw money, but withdrawals should throw an exception if there are insufficient funds.

Requirements

1. **Deposit**: Adds money to the balance.

2. **Withdraw**: Deducts money from the balance but throws an InsufficientBalanceException if there's not enough money.

3. **Display Balance**: Shows the current balance.

Implementation

1. Create the Custom Exception

java

```java
public class InsufficientBalanceException extends Exception {
    public InsufficientBalanceException(String message) {
        super(message);
    }
}
```

2. Create the BankAccount Class

java

```java
public class BankAccount {
    private double balance;

    public BankAccount(double initialBalance) {
        balance = initialBalance;
    }

    public void deposit(double amount) {
```

```java
        if (amount > 0) {
            balance += amount;
        }
    }


    public void withdraw(double amount) throws
InsufficientBalanceException {
        if (amount > balance) {
            throw new
InsufficientBalanceException("Insufficient funds for
withdrawal.");
        }
        balance -= amount;
    }


    public double getBalance() {
        return balance;
    }
}
```

3. **Main Class for User Interaction**

java

```java
import java.util.Scanner;

public class Main {
    public static void main(String[] args) {
        BankAccount account = new BankAccount(100);
        // Initial balance of 100
        Scanner scanner = new Scanner(System.in);

        System.out.println("Bank Account Management");

        while (true) {
            System.out.println("\n1. Deposit");
            System.out.println("2. Withdraw");
            System.out.println("3. Show Balance");
            System.out.println("4. Exit");
            System.out.print("Choose an option: ");
            int choice = scanner.nextInt();

            switch (choice) {
                case 1:
```

```java
                System.out.print("Enter deposit amount: ");

                double deposit = scanner.nextDouble();

                account.deposit(deposit);

                System.out.println("Deposited " + deposit);

                break;


            case 2:

                System.out.print("Enter withdrawal amount: ");

                double withdraw = scanner.nextDouble();

                try {

                    account.withdraw(withdraw);

                    System.out.println("Withdrew " + withdraw);

                } catch (InsufficientBalanceException e) {

                    System.out.println(e.getMessage());

                }

                break;


            case 3:
```

```java
                System.out.println("Current balance: " +
account.getBalance());

                break;


        case 4:

            System.out.println("Exiting...");

            scanner.close();

            return;


        default:

            System.out.println("Invalid option. Try
again.");

                break;
            }
        }
    }
}
```

Explanation

- **Custom Exception**:
  InsufficientBalanceException provides a
  descriptive error when withdrawal conditions
  aren't met.

- **try-catch Block**: Handles exceptions in the withdrawal process, preventing program crashes.

- **User Interaction**: Allows users to deposit, withdraw, or view their balance in a looped menu format.

Conclusion

In this chapter, you learned how to handle exceptions in Java using try, catch, finally, throw, and throws. You also explored essential debugging techniques such as setting breakpoints and using watch expressions to trace errors. By implementing exception handling and debugging techniques, you're now equipped to write more resilient Java applications and identify errors effectively.

In the next chapter, we'll explore Java's Input and Output (I/O) capabilities, enabling you to read from and write to files, work with data streams, and manage resources efficiently.

Chapter 6: Working with Java I/O (Input/Output)

Introduction to Java I/O

Input and output operations are fundamental in programming, allowing applications to interact with the outside world. Java's I/O package (java.io) provides classes and interfaces to perform I/O operations, including reading from and writing to files, handling byte and character streams, and managing resources. In this chapter, we'll look at the basics of file handling, explore the differences between byte and character streams, and learn how to handle data efficiently.

6.1 Overview of Java I/O Classes

Java's I/O API includes several core classes and interfaces to handle data:

1. **File**: Represents a file or directory path.

2. **Streams**: Used to read and write data in bytes or characters.

3. **Reader and Writer**: Specialized classes for reading and writing character data.

Java I/O classes are divided into two main types:

- **Byte Streams**: Handle raw binary data, commonly used for files, images, and binary files. They include classes like InputStream and OutputStream.

- **Character Streams**: Handle character data, typically used for text files. They include classes like Reader and Writer.

6.2 Working with the File Class

The File class represents a file or directory path. It doesn't read or write data itself but provides methods to work with files and directories.

Creating and Checking a File

java

```
import java.io.File;

import java.io.IOException;
```

```java
public class FileExample {
    public static void main(String[] args) {
        File file = new File("example.txt");
        try {
            if (file.createNewFile()) {
                System.out.println("File created: " +
file.getName());
            } else {
                System.out.println("File already exists.");
            }
        } catch (IOException e) {
            System.out.println("An error occurred.");
            e.printStackTrace();
        }
    }
}
```

- **createNewFile()**: Creates a new file and returns true if successful.

- **exists()**: Checks if the file or directory already exists.

- **delete()**: Deletes the file or directory.

Checking File Properties

java

```
System.out.println("File name: " + file.getName());

System.out.println("Absolute path: " +
file.getAbsolutePath());

System.out.println("Writable: " + file.canWrite());

System.out.println("Readable: " + file.canRead());

System.out.println("File size: " + file.length() + "
bytes");
```

These methods provide useful information about the file, such as its path, readability, writability, and size.

6.3 Byte Streams

Byte streams read and write data in bytes, making them ideal for handling binary data, such as images or audio files. The two main classes are FileInputStream and FileOutputStream.

Reading Files with FileInputStream

FileInputStream reads raw byte data from a file.

java

```java
import java.io.FileInputStream;

import java.io.IOException;


public class ByteStreamReadExample {

    public static void main(String[] args) {

        try (FileInputStream fis = new
FileInputStream("example.txt")) {

            int content;

            while ((content = fis.read()) != -1) {

                System.out.print((char) content);

            }

        } catch (IOException e) {

            e.printStackTrace();

        }

    }

}
```

- **read()**: Reads a byte of data and returns -1 when the end of the file is reached.

- **try-with-resources**: Automatically closes the stream after operations, ensuring no resource leaks.

Writing Files with FileOutputStream

FileOutputStream writes raw byte data to a file.

java

```java
import java.io.FileOutputStream;
import java.io.IOException;

public class ByteStreamWriteExample {
    public static void main(String[] args) {
        String content = "Hello, Java I/O!";
        try (FileOutputStream fos = new FileOutputStream("output.txt")) {
            fos.write(content.getBytes());
            System.out.println("Data written to file.");
        } catch (IOException e) {
            e.printStackTrace();
        }
    }
}
```

- **write()**: Writes a byte array to the file, useful for saving strings or binary data.

6.4 Character Streams

Character streams are specialized for text data and handle character encoding automatically, making them ideal for working with text files. The main classes are FileReader and FileWriter.

Reading Files with FileReader

FileReader reads character data from a file.

java

```
import java.io.FileReader;

import java.io.IOException;


public class CharacterStreamReadExample {
    public static void main(String[] args) {
        try (FileReader reader = new FileReader("example.txt")) {
            int character;
            while ((character = reader.read()) != -1) {
                System.out.print((char) character);
            }
        } catch (IOException e) {
            e.printStackTrace();
```

```
        }
    }
}
```

Writing Files with FileWriter

FileWriter writes character data to a file.

java

```java
import java.io.FileWriter;
import java.io.IOException;

public class CharacterStreamWriteExample {
    public static void main(String[] args) {
        String content = "Hello, Java Character Stream!";
        try (FileWriter writer = new
FileWriter("output.txt")) {
            writer.write(content);
            System.out.println("Data written to file.");
        } catch (IOException e) {
            e.printStackTrace();
        }
    }
```

}

In both examples, the try-with-resources statement is used to close the streams automatically, a best practice to avoid resource leaks.

6.5 Buffered Streams

Buffered streams improve I/O performance by reducing the number of read/write operations. They read/write data in larger chunks and are often used in conjunction with FileReader and FileWriter.

BufferedReader and BufferedWriter

BufferedReader and BufferedWriter read and write text data with enhanced efficiency.

java

```java
import java.io.BufferedReader;

import java.io.FileReader;

import java.io.IOException;


public class BufferedReaderExample {
    public static void main(String[] args) {
```

```java
    try (BufferedReader reader = new
BufferedReader(new FileReader("example.txt"))) {

        String line;

        while ((line = reader.readLine()) != null) {

            System.out.println(line);

        }

    } catch (IOException e) {

        e.printStackTrace();

    }

}
```

- **readLine()**: Reads an entire line of text, returning null when the end of the file is reached.

6.6 Serialization and Deserialization

Serialization is the process of converting an object into a byte stream, allowing it to be saved to a file or transmitted over a network. Deserialization is the reverse, reconstructing the object from the byte stream. To make a class serializable, implement the Serializable interface.

Serialization Example

java

```java
import java.io.FileOutputStream;
import java.io.ObjectOutputStream;
import java.io.Serializable;
import java.io.IOException;

public class Person implements Serializable {
    private static final long serialVersionUID = 1L;
    private String name;
    private int age;

    public Person(String name, int age) {
        this.name = name;
        this.age = age;
    }

    public static void main(String[] args) {
        Person person = new Person("Alice", 30);
```

```java
    try (ObjectOutputStream oos = new
ObjectOutputStream(new
FileOutputStream("person.ser"))) {

        oos.writeObject(person);

        System.out.println("Person object serialized.");

    } catch (IOException e) {

        e.printStackTrace();

    }

  }

}
```

Deserialization Example

java

```java
import java.io.FileInputStream;

import java.io.ObjectInputStream;

import java.io.IOException;


public class DeserializePerson {

  public static void main(String[] args) {

    try (ObjectInputStream ois = new
ObjectInputStream(new
FileInputStream("person.ser"))) {
```

```java
        Person person = (Person) ois.readObject();

        System.out.println("Deserialized Person: " +
person.getName() + ", Age: " + person.getAge());

    } catch (IOException | ClassNotFoundException
e) {

        e.printStackTrace();

    }

  }

}
```

This example serializes a Person object to a file and then deserializes it to recreate the object.

6.7 Project: Simple File-Based To-Do List Application

In this project, we'll create a simple console-based to-do list application that uses Java I/O to save tasks to a file and retrieve them on-demand. The application will:

1. Add tasks to a to-do list.

2. View all tasks.

3. Save tasks to a file.

4. Load tasks from a file.

Step 1: Define the Task Class

java

```java
import java.io.Serializable;

public class Task implements Serializable {
    private static final long serialVersionUID = 1L;
    private String description;

    public Task(String description) {
        this.description = description;
    }

    public String getDescription() {
        return description;
    }

    @Override
    public String toString() {
        return description;
    }
}
```

}

Step 2: TaskManager Class for Managing Tasks

java

```java
import java.util.ArrayList;
import java.io.*;

public class TaskManager {
    private ArrayList<Task> tasks = new ArrayList<>();
    private static final String FILE_NAME = "tasks.ser";

    public void addTask(Task task) {
        tasks.add(task);
    }

    public void viewTasks() {
        if (tasks.isEmpty()) {
            System.out.println("No tasks available.");
        } else {
```

```java
        tasks.forEach(System.out::println);

    }
}


    public void saveTasks() {
        try (ObjectOutputStream oos = new
ObjectOutputStream(new
FileOutputStream(FILE_NAME))) {

            oos.writeObject(tasks);

            System.out.println("Tasks saved
successfully.");

        } catch (IOException e) {

            e.printStackTrace();

        }
    }


    public void loadTasks() {
        try (ObjectInputStream ois = new
ObjectInputStream(new
FileInputStream(FILE_NAME))) {

            tasks = (ArrayList<Task>) ois.readObject();

            System.out.println("Tasks loaded
successfully.");
```

```java
        } catch (IOException | ClassNotFoundException
e) {

            System.out.println("No saved tasks found.");

        }

    }

}
```

Step 3: Main Class for User Interaction

java

```java
import java.util.Scanner;

public class Main {
    public static void main(String[] args) {
        TaskManager manager = new TaskManager();
        Scanner scanner = new Scanner(System.in);

        while (true) {
            System.out.println("\n1. Add Task");
            System.out.println("2. View Tasks");
            System.out.println("3. Save Tasks");
            System.out.println("4. Load Tasks");
```

```java
System.out.println("5. Exit");
System.out.print("Choose an option: ");
int choice = scanner.nextInt();
scanner.nextLine(); // Clear buffer

switch (choice) {
    case 1:
        System.out.print("Enter task description: ");
        String description = scanner.nextLine();
        manager.addTask(new Task(description));
        break;

    case 2:
        manager.viewTasks();
        break;

    case 3:
        manager.saveTasks();
        break;
```

```java
            case 4:

                manager.loadTasks();

                break;


            case 5:

                System.out.println("Exiting...");

                scanner.close();

                return;


            default:

                System.out.println("Invalid option.");

                break;

        }

      }

    }

}
```

This simple to-do list application demonstrates the practical use of serialization and I/O operations to save and load tasks. It also uses an ArrayList to manage multiple Task objects, showcasing the flexibility of Java collections and I/O.

Conclusion

In this chapter, you learned about Java's I/O API, including the File class, byte and character streams, buffered streams, and serialization. You also implemented a file-based to-do list application that saves and retrieves tasks, demonstrating how Java I/O can be applied in a real-world context.

In the next chapter, we'll explore multithreading and concurrency in Java, enabling you to write programs that can perform multiple tasks simultaneously, boosting performance and responsiveness.

Chapter 7: Multithreading and Concurrency in Java

Introduction to Multithreading

Multithreading is the ability of a CPU or a single process to execute multiple threads concurrently. A **thread** is the smallest unit of a process, executing instructions independently. By using multiple threads, applications can perform background tasks, handle multiple user requests, or split work across cores in a multi-core CPU, leading to better performance and user experience.

Java's support for multithreading is built into the language, making it an ideal choice for building concurrent applications.

7.1 Understanding Threads in Java

In Java, threads can be created in two main ways:

1. **Extending the Thread class**.

2. **Implementing the Runnable interface**.

Each approach has its own use cases, and the choice depends on the requirements and design of the application.

Creating Threads by Extending the Thread Class

To create a thread by extending the Thread class, override the run() method with the code you want the thread to execute.

java

```
public class MyThread extends Thread {

    @Override

    public void run() {

        for (int i = 1; i <= 5; i++) {

            System.out.println("Thread: " + i);

            try {

                Thread.sleep(500); // Pauses execution for 500 milliseconds

            } catch (InterruptedException e) {
```

```java
            e.printStackTrace();

        }

      }

    }

  }
```

```java
public class Main {

    public static void main(String[] args) {

        MyThread thread = new MyThread();

        thread.start(); // Starts the thread, calling the run()
method

    }

}
```

- **start()**: Begins execution of the thread, calling the run() method.

- **sleep()**: Pauses the thread for a specified time, releasing the CPU for other tasks.

Creating Threads by Implementing Runnable

Another way to create threads is by implementing the Runnable interface, which is more flexible as it allows you to extend other classes if needed.

java

```java
public class MyRunnable implements Runnable {
    @Override
    public void run() {
        for (int i = 1; i <= 5; i++) {
            System.out.println("Runnable: " + i);
            try {
                Thread.sleep(500);
            } catch (InterruptedException e) {
                e.printStackTrace();
            }
        }
    }
}


public class Main {
    public static void main(String[] args) {
        Thread thread = new Thread(new MyRunnable());
        thread.start();
    }
}
```

Using Runnable is often preferred in Java because it promotes composition over inheritance and allows greater flexibility.

7.2 Lifecycle of a Thread

A Java thread has several states, defined by the Thread.State enumeration:

- **NEW**: The thread is created but has not yet started.

- **RUNNABLE**: The thread is ready to run or is currently running.

- **BLOCKED**: The thread is waiting for a monitor lock to enter or re-enter a synchronized block or method.

- **WAITING**: The thread is waiting indefinitely for another thread to perform a specific action (e.g., using wait()).

- **TIMED_WAITING**: The thread is waiting for a specified amount of time (e.g., using sleep()).

- **TERMINATED**: The thread has completed execution.

Understanding these states helps you troubleshoot and optimize thread behavior in complex applications.

7.3 Synchronization and Thread Safety

When multiple threads access shared resources, data consistency and integrity can become an issue. Java provides synchronization mechanisms to ensure that only one thread accesses a resource at a time.

Synchronized Methods

A synchronized method allows only one thread to execute at a time on the same object.

java

```java
public class Counter {
    private int count = 0;

    public synchronized void increment() {
        count++;
    }

    public int getCount() {
        return count;
    }
}
```

In this example, only one thread can execute increment() at a time, ensuring thread safety for the count variable.

Synchronized Blocks

Sometimes you only need to synchronize a specific block of code rather than an entire method. Synchronized blocks are more efficient and help reduce lock contention.

java

```java
public class Counter {
    private int count = 0;

    public void increment() {
        synchronized (this) {
            count++;
        }
    }

    public int getCount() {
        return count;
    }
}
```

```
}
```

Using Locks

Java provides the Lock interface and classes like ReentrantLock to provide more flexibility than synchronized methods and blocks. Lock allows finer control over thread locking, such as timed locking.

java

```java
import java.util.concurrent.locks.ReentrantLock;

public class Counter {
    private int count = 0;
    private final ReentrantLock lock = new ReentrantLock();

    public void increment() {
        lock.lock();
        try {
            count++;
        } finally {
            lock.unlock();
        }
```

```
}

    public int getCount() {

        return count;

    }

}
```

Locks give more control over synchronization and should be used carefully to avoid deadlocks.

7.4 Inter-Thread Communication

Inter-thread communication is useful when threads need to cooperate to complete a task. Java provides wait(), notify(), and notifyAll() methods to coordinate threads, allowing them to notify each other when certain conditions are met.

Using wait() and notify()

The wait() method pauses a thread until another thread calls notify() or notifyAll() on the same object.

java

```java
public class SharedResource {
    private int value = 0;
```

```java
private boolean hasValue = false;

public synchronized void produce(int newValue) {
    while (hasValue) {
        try {
            wait(); // Waits until the value is consumed
        } catch (InterruptedException e) {
            e.printStackTrace();
        }
    }
    value = newValue;
    hasValue = true;
    System.out.println("Produced: " + value);
    notify(); // Notifies consumer
}

public synchronized void consume() {
    while (!hasValue) {
        try {
            wait(); // Waits until a value is produced
        } catch (InterruptedException e) {
```

```java
                e.printStackTrace();

        }

    }

    System.out.println("Consumed: " + value);

    hasValue = false;

    notify(); // Notifies producer

    }

}
```

In this example, produce() waits if there is already a value, while consume() waits if there is no value, ensuring proper coordination.

7.5 The Executor Framework

The Executor framework provides a high-level API for managing threads and asynchronous tasks. Instead of creating and managing individual threads, you can use an ExecutorService to manage a pool of threads, which is more efficient and scalable.

Creating a Fixed-Thread Pool

java

```java
import java.util.concurrent.ExecutorService;
```

```java
import java.util.concurrent.Executors;

public class ExecutorExample {
    public static void main(String[] args) {
        ExecutorService executor =
Executors.newFixedThreadPool(3);

        for (int i = 0; i < 5; i++) {
            executor.submit(() -> {
                System.out.println("Executing task by " +
Thread.currentThread().getName());
            });
        }
        executor.shutdown();
    }
}
```

In this example, a pool of three threads handles five tasks, reusing threads instead of creating new ones each time.

ScheduledExecutorService

The ScheduledExecutorService allows you to schedule tasks to run periodically or after a delay.

java

```java
import java.util.concurrent.Executors;
import java.util.concurrent.ScheduledExecutorService;
import java.util.concurrent.TimeUnit;

public class ScheduledExecutorExample {
    public static void main(String[] args) {
        ScheduledExecutorService scheduler =
Executors.newScheduledThreadPool(2);

        scheduler.scheduleAtFixedRate(() -> {
            System.out.println("Scheduled task executed at
" + System.currentTimeMillis());
        }, 0, 2, TimeUnit.SECONDS);
    }
}
```

This example schedules a task to execute every 2 seconds.

7.6 Concurrency Utilities

Java's java.util.concurrent package provides a range of utilities that simplify concurrent programming.

CountDownLatch

CountDownLatch allows one or more threads to wait until a set of operations complete.

java

```java
import java.util.concurrent.CountDownLatch;

public class CountDownLatchExample {
    public static void main(String[] args) throws InterruptedException {
        CountDownLatch latch = new CountDownLatch(3);

        for (int i = 0; i < 3; i++) {
            new Thread(() -> {
                System.out.println("Task completed by " + Thread.currentThread().getName());
```

```java
            latch.countDown();
        }).start();
    }

        latch.await(); // Waits until the count reaches 0
        System.out.println("All tasks completed.");
    }
}
```

CyclicBarrier

CyclicBarrier lets multiple threads wait until a common point before proceeding.

java

```java
import java.util.concurrent.CyclicBarrier;

public class CyclicBarrierExample {
    public static void main(String[] args) {
        CyclicBarrier barrier = new CyclicBarrier(3, () ->
{
            System.out.println("All threads reached the barrier, proceeding...");
        });
```

```java
for (int i = 0; i < 3; i++) {

    new Thread(() -> {

        try {

System.out.println(Thread.currentThread().getName()
+ " waiting at barrier.");

            barrier.await(); // Waits until all threads
reach the barrier
        } catch (Exception e) {

            e.printStackTrace();

        }

    }).start();

}

}
```

These utilities make it easier to manage complex synchronization requirements.

7.7 Project: Multi-Threaded File Processor

To apply these concepts, let's create a simple multi-threaded file processor. This program will read lines from multiple files concurrently and process them.

Project Requirements

1. **Read multiple files in parallel.**
2. **Count occurrences of a specific word in each file.**
3. **Display results for each file and total word count across all files.**

Step 1: FileProcessor Class

java

```
import java.io.BufferedReader;

import java.io.FileReader;

import java.io.IOException;

import java.util.concurrent.Callable;


public class FileProcessor implements
Callable<Integer> {

    private String filePath;
```

```java
    private String targetWord;


    public FileProcessor(String filePath, String
targetWord) {
        this.filePath = filePath;

        this.targetWord = targetWord;

    }


    @Override
    public Integer call() {
        int count = 0;

        try (BufferedReader reader = new
BufferedReader(new FileReader(filePath))) {
            String line;

            while ((line = reader.readLine()) != null) {

                count += line.split(targetWord, -1).length -
1;

            }

        } catch (IOException e) {
            e.printStackTrace();

        }

        return count;
```

```
    }
}
```

Step 2: Main Class with Executor Service

java

```java
import java.util.ArrayList;
import java.util.List;
import java.util.concurrent.ExecutionException;
import java.util.concurrent.ExecutorService;
import java.util.concurrent.Executors;
import java.util.concurrent.Future;

public class Main {
    public static void main(String[] args) {
        String[] files = {"file1.txt", "file2.txt",
"file3.txt"};
        String targetWord = "Java";

        ExecutorService executor =
Executors.newFixedThreadPool(files.length);
        List<Future<Integer>> results = new
ArrayList<>();
```

```java
        for (String file : files) {

            FileProcessor task = new FileProcessor(file,
targetWord);

            results.add(executor.submit(task));

        }


        int totalOccurrences = 0;

        for (Future<Integer> result : results) {

            try {

                totalOccurrences += result.get();

            } catch (InterruptedException |
ExecutionException e) {

                e.printStackTrace();

            }

        }


        System.out.println("Total occurrences of '" +
targetWord + "': " + totalOccurrences);

        executor.shutdown();

    }

}
```

This project demonstrates how to use ExecutorService to process files concurrently, improving efficiency.

Conclusion

In this chapter, you learned the basics of multithreading and concurrency in Java, including thread creation, synchronization, inter-thread communication, and the Executor framework. You also implemented a multi-threaded file processor project to apply these concepts in a real-world scenario. By mastering multithreading, you can build high-performance applications that handle multiple tasks concurrently.

In the next chapter, we'll explore Java's networking capabilities, enabling you to develop applications that communicate over the internet or a local network.

Chapter 8: Java Networking and APIs

Introduction to Networking in Java

Networking allows applications to communicate with each other, either on the same machine or over the internet. Java provides robust APIs for networking, allowing developers to create everything from simple client-server programs to complex applications that interact with remote servers via HTTP. Understanding Java's networking capabilities is essential for building applications that share data or rely on remote services, such as retrieving data from web APIs or enabling real-time communication.

8.1 Java's Networking API Basics

Java's networking API is part of the java.net package, which provides classes and interfaces for:

- **Sockets**: For establishing connections between devices.

- **URLs**: For accessing and processing data over the web.

- **Datagrams**: For sending and receiving packets without establishing a connection.

- **HTTP**: For interacting with web services.

These tools make it easy to implement both low-level network communication (using sockets) and high-level communication (like making HTTP requests).

8.2 Working with Sockets

Sockets are endpoints for communication between two machines over a network. Java supports two primary types of sockets:

1. **TCP (Transmission Control Protocol)**: A connection-oriented protocol that ensures reliable data transmission between sender and receiver.

2. **UDP (User Datagram Protocol)**: A connectionless protocol that sends packets without guaranteeing delivery, often used for time-sensitive applications like streaming.

Creating a TCP Client-Server Application

A simple client-server application allows a server to listen for requests from clients and respond accordingly. In Java, this is done using ServerSocket (for servers) and Socket (for clients).

Server Code Example

java

```java
import java.io.*;
import java.net.*;

public class Server {
    public static void main(String[] args) {
        try (ServerSocket serverSocket = new ServerSocket(8080)) {
            System.out.println("Server started. Waiting for clients...");
            while (true) {
                Socket clientSocket = serverSocket.accept();
                System.out.println("Client connected.");
                BufferedReader reader = new BufferedReader(new InputStreamReader(clientSocket.getInputStream()));
                PrintWriter writer = new PrintWriter(clientSocket.getOutputStream(), true);
```

```java
            String clientMessage = reader.readLine();

            System.out.println("Received from client: "
+ clientMessage);

            writer.println("Hello from Server!");

            clientSocket.close();

        }

    } catch (IOException e) {

        e.printStackTrace();

    }

  }

}
```

Client Code Example

java

```java
import java.io.*;
import java.net.*;


public class Client {
    public static void main(String[] args) {

        try (Socket socket = new Socket("localhost",
8080)) {
```

```java
        PrintWriter writer = new
PrintWriter(socket.getOutputStream(), true);

        BufferedReader reader = new
BufferedReader(new
InputStreamReader(socket.getInputStream()));


        writer.println("Hello, Server!");

        String serverResponse = reader.readLine();

        System.out.println("Received from server: " +
serverResponse);

    } catch (IOException e) {

        e.printStackTrace();

    }

  }

}
```

In this example:

- The server listens on port 8080 and waits for client connections.

- The client connects to the server, sends a message, and receives a response.

- Both server and client use input and output streams to communicate.

Creating a UDP Client-Server Application

UDP applications send data packets (datagrams) without establishing a dedicated connection. This approach is faster but doesn't guarantee packet delivery.

UDP Server Example

java

```java
import java.net.*;

public class UDPServer {
    public static void main(String[] args) {
        try (DatagramSocket socket = new DatagramSocket(8080)) {
            byte[] buffer = new byte[256];
            DatagramPacket packet = new DatagramPacket(buffer, buffer.length);

            System.out.println("UDP server waiting for packets...");
            socket.receive(packet);
            String received = new String(packet.getData(), 0, packet.getLength());
            System.out.println("Received: " + received);
```

```java
        } catch (Exception e) {
            e.printStackTrace();
        }
    }
}
```

UDP Client Example

java

```java
import java.net.*;

public class UDPClient {
    public static void main(String[] args) {
        try (DatagramSocket socket = new DatagramSocket()) {
            byte[] buffer = "Hello UDP Server".getBytes();
            InetAddress address = InetAddress.getByName("localhost");
            DatagramPacket packet = new DatagramPacket(buffer, buffer.length, address, 8080);

            socket.send(packet);
```

```
        System.out.println("Message sent to UDP
server.");

    } catch (Exception e) {

        e.printStackTrace();

    }

  }

}
```

In this UDP example, the client sends a datagram packet to the server, which then receives it and prints the message. Unlike TCP, UDP doesn't guarantee message order or delivery.

8.3 Working with URLs

Java provides the URL class to represent web addresses and fetch resources over HTTP and HTTPS.

Creating a URL Object

You can create a URL object by passing a valid URL string to its constructor:

java

```
import java.net.*;
```

```java
public class URLExample {

    public static void main(String[] args) {

        try {

            URL url = new
URL("https://www.example.com");

            System.out.println("Protocol: " +
url.getProtocol());

            System.out.println("Host: " + url.getHost());

            System.out.println("File: " + url.getFile());

            System.out.println("Port: " + url.getPort());

        } catch (MalformedURLException e) {

            e.printStackTrace();

        }

    }

}
```

The URL class provides methods to retrieve information about the URL, such as its protocol, host, and file path.

Reading Data from a URL

You can open an InputStream on a URL object to read data from it.

java

```java
import java.io.*;

import java.net.*;


public class URLReader {

    public static void main(String[] args) {

        try {

            URL url = new
URL("https://www.example.com");

            BufferedReader reader = new
BufferedReader(new
InputStreamReader(url.openStream()));

            String line;

            while ((line = reader.readLine()) != null) {

                System.out.println(line);

            }

            reader.close();

        } catch (IOException e) {

            e.printStackTrace();

        }

    }

}
```

This example reads the HTML content of a webpage and prints it to the console.

8.4 Working with HTTP and Web APIs

Modern applications often communicate with remote servers using HTTP to exchange data. In Java, you can use the HttpURLConnection class or libraries like **Apache HttpClient** or **OkHttp** to interact with web APIs.

Using HttpURLConnection

The HttpURLConnection class allows you to send HTTP GET and POST requests and handle the responses.

Sending a GET Request

java

```java
import java.io.*;
import java.net.*;


public class HttpGetExample {
    public static void main(String[] args) {
```

```java
try {
    URL url = new
URL("https://jsonplaceholder.typicode.com/posts/1");
    HttpURLConnection connection =
(HttpURLConnection) url.openConnection();
    connection.setRequestMethod("GET");

    int responseCode =
connection.getResponseCode();
    System.out.println("Response Code: " +
responseCode);

    if (responseCode ==
HttpURLConnection.HTTP_OK) {
        BufferedReader in = new
BufferedReader(new
InputStreamReader(connection.getInputStream()));
        String line;
        while ((line = in.readLine()) != null) {
            System.out.println(line);
        }
        in.close();
    }
```

```java
        } catch (IOException e) {
            e.printStackTrace();
        }
    }
}
```

This code sends a GET request to a sample API and prints the JSON response.

Sending a POST Request

java

```java
import java.io.*;
import java.net.*;

public class HttpPostExample {
    public static void main(String[] args) {
        try {
            URL url = new
URL("https://jsonplaceholder.typicode.com/posts");
            HttpURLConnection connection =
(HttpURLConnection) url.openConnection();
            connection.setRequestMethod("POST");
```

```java
        connection.setRequestProperty("Content-Type", "application/json");

        connection.setDoOutput(true);


        String jsonInputString =
"{\"title\":\"foo\",\"body\":\"bar\",\"userId\":1}";


        try (OutputStream os =
connection.getOutputStream()) {
                byte[] input = jsonInputString.getBytes("utf-8");

                os.write(input, 0, input.length);

        }


        int responseCode =
connection.getResponseCode();
        System.out.println("Response Code: " +
responseCode);


        if (responseCode ==
HttpURLConnection.HTTP_CREATED) {
                BufferedReader in = new
BufferedReader(new
InputStreamReader(connection.getInputStream()));
```

```java
        String line;

        while ((line = in.readLine()) != null) {

            System.out.println(line);

        }

        in.close();

    }

} catch (IOException e) {

    e.printStackTrace();

}

}

}
```

This code sends a POST request with JSON data to the server and retrieves the server's response.

8.5 Parsing JSON Responses

Java doesn't provide a built-in library for parsing JSON, but popular libraries like **org.json** and **Gson** can help.

Parsing JSON with org.json

java

```java
import org.json.JSONObject;

public class JsonExample {
    public static void main(String[] args) {
        String json = "{\"name\":\"John\",\"age\":30}";
        JSONObject jsonObject = new JSONObject(json);
        System.out.println("Name: " + jsonObject.getString("name"));
        System.out.println("Age: " + jsonObject.getInt("age"));
    }
}
```

Parsing JSON with Gson

java

```java
import com.google.gson.Gson;

public class GsonExample {
    public static void main(String[] args) {
        String json = "{\"name\":\"Jane\",\"age\":25}";
        Gson gson = new Gson();
```

```java
        Person person = gson.fromJson(json,
Person.class);

        System.out.println("Name: " +
person.getName());

        System.out.println("Age: " + person.getAge());

    }

}


class Person {

    private String name;

    private int age;


    public String getName() { return name; }

    public int getAge() { return age; }

}
```

Both libraries parse JSON data into Java objects, making it easy to handle API responses.

8.6 Project: Simple Weather Application Using OpenWeatherMap API

Let's build a simple weather application that fetches weather data from the OpenWeatherMap API and displays it to the user.

Project Requirements

1. **Fetch current weather data for a city.**

2. **Display temperature, humidity, and description.**

3. **Parse the JSON response to extract necessary information.**

Step 1: Fetch Weather Data

java

```java
import java.io.*;
import java.net.*;


public class WeatherFetcher {
    private static final String API_KEY = "your_api_key";
```

```java
    private static final String BASE_URL =
"https://api.openweathermap.org/data/2.5/weather?q="
;


    public String fetchWeather(String city) {
        String urlString = BASE_URL + city +
"&appid=" + API_KEY + "&units=metric";
        StringBuilder result = new StringBuilder();


        try {
            URL url = new URL(urlString);
            HttpURLConnection connection =
(HttpURLConnection) url.openConnection();
            connection.setRequestMethod("GET");


            BufferedReader reader = new
BufferedReader(new
InputStreamReader(connection.getInputStream()));
            String line;
            while ((line = reader.readLine()) != null) {
                result.append(line);
            }
            reader.close();
```

```java
        } catch (IOException e) {
            e.printStackTrace();
        }
        return result.toString();
    }
}
```

Step 2: Parse and Display Weather Data

Using org.json to parse JSON data:

java

```java
import org.json.JSONObject;

public class WeatherParser {
    public void parseAndDisplay(String json) {
        JSONObject jsonObject = new JSONObject(json);
        JSONObject main = jsonObject.getJSONObject("main");
        double temperature = main.getDouble("temp");
        int humidity = main.getInt("humidity");
```

```java
        String description =
jsonObject.getJSONArray("weather").getJSONObject(
0).getString("description");


        System.out.println("Temperature: " + temperature
+ "°C");

        System.out.println("Humidity: " + humidity +
"%");

        System.out.println("Description: " + description);

    }

}
```

Step 3: Main Class for User Interaction

java

```java
import java.util.Scanner;


public class Main {
    public static void main(String[] args) {
        WeatherFetcher fetcher = new WeatherFetcher();
        WeatherParser parser = new WeatherParser();
        Scanner scanner = new Scanner(System.in);
```

```
System.out.print("Enter city: ");

String city = scanner.nextLine();

String weatherData = fetcher.fetchWeather(city);

parser.parseAndDisplay(weatherData);


scanner.close();

    }

}
```

This simple project demonstrates how to fetch, parse, and display data from a web API, providing a useful way to build practical applications using Java networking and APIs.

Conclusion

In this chapter, you learned the basics of networking in Java, including socket programming, URL handling, and HTTP communication with HttpURLConnection. You also explored JSON parsing and applied these skills to build a simple weather application using the OpenWeatherMap API. These skills are essential for building applications that interact with remote servers or third-party APIs, making your applications more dynamic and connected.

In the next chapter, we'll delve into graphical user interface (GUI) development using JavaFX, allowing you to create interactive applications with a visual interface.

Chapter 9: GUI Development with JavaFX

Introduction to JavaFX

JavaFX is Java's flagship framework for creating rich, interactive desktop applications. It provides a robust API to design applications with graphical interfaces and supports features like animations, media playback, and custom styling with CSS. JavaFX applications can run on various platforms, including Windows, macOS, and Linux, making it a versatile choice for desktop development.

In this chapter, we'll explore JavaFX's basic structure, learn how to build a simple GUI, and develop a practical project to apply these skills.

9.1 Setting Up JavaFX

To get started with JavaFX, you need to ensure that JavaFX libraries are included in your development environment. Here's how to set it up.

Step 1: Download JavaFX SDK

1. Download the JavaFX SDK from Gluon's official site.

2. Extract the SDK and note the installation path, as you'll need it to configure your IDE.

Step 2: Configure Your IDE

Most IDEs, such as IntelliJ IDEA or Eclipse, provide options to add JavaFX libraries to your project. Here's an example setup for IntelliJ IDEA:

1. Go to **File > Project Structure**.

2. Select **Libraries** and add the extracted JavaFX library files.

3. For running JavaFX applications, you may need to add VM options to your Run Configuration:

plaintext

```
--module-path "path_to_javafx_lib" --add-modules javafx.controls,javafx.fxml
```

9.2 JavaFX Application Structure

Every JavaFX application must extend the Application class and override its start() method. The start() method is the main entry point for JavaFX applications and provides a Stage object, which represents the primary window.

Basic JavaFX Application Example

java

```
import javafx.application.Application;

import javafx.scene.Scene;

import javafx.scene.control.Label;

import javafx.stage.Stage;


public class HelloWorldApp extends Application {
    @Override
    public void start(Stage primaryStage) {
        Label label = new Label("Hello, JavaFX!");
        Scene scene = new Scene(label, 300, 200);

        primaryStage.setTitle("Hello World");
        primaryStage.setScene(scene);
        primaryStage.show();
    }
```

```
public static void main(String[] args) {

    launch(args); // Launches the JavaFX application

}

}
```

In this example:

- **Stage**: Represents the main application window.

- **Scene**: Contains all the UI elements (nodes).

- **Label**: A simple text component.

The launch() method starts the JavaFX application, and primaryStage.show() displays the window.

9.3 JavaFX Layouts

JavaFX uses layout managers to organize UI components. Layouts control the positioning and sizing of nodes within the GUI.

Common Layouts in JavaFX

1. **HBox**: A horizontal layout container.

2. **VBox**: A vertical layout container.

3. **BorderPane**: Divides the window into five regions (top, bottom, left, right, and center).

4. **GridPane**: Arranges nodes in a flexible grid of rows and columns.

Example of a basic layout with VBox and HBox:

java

```
import javafx.application.Application;

import javafx.scene.Scene;

import javafx.scene.control.Button;

import javafx.scene.layout.VBox;

import javafx.stage.Stage;


public class LayoutExample extends Application {
    @Override
    public void start(Stage primaryStage) {
        VBox vbox = new VBox(10); // Vertical layout
with 10px spacing
        Button button1 = new Button("Button 1");
        Button button2 = new Button("Button 2");

        vbox.getChildren().addAll(button1, button2);
        Scene scene = new Scene(vbox, 200, 100);
```

```
    primaryStage.setTitle("VBox Layout Example");

    primaryStage.setScene(scene);

    primaryStage.show();

}


public static void main(String[] args) {

    launch(args);

}

}
```

In this example, the VBox layout manager places buttons vertically. HBox works similarly but arranges nodes horizontally.

9.4 JavaFX Controls

JavaFX provides various controls for building interactive applications, including buttons, text fields, checkboxes, and more. Here are some commonly used controls:

Button

A button triggers an action when clicked.

```java
Button button = new Button("Click Me");
button.setOnAction(event ->
System.out.println("Button Clicked!"));
```

TextField

A text field allows users to enter text.

```java
TextField textField = new TextField();
textField.setPromptText("Enter your name");
```

Checkbox

Checkboxes let users select options.

```java
CheckBox checkBox = new CheckBox("Accept Terms");
checkBox.setOnAction(event -> {
    if (checkBox.isSelected()) {
        System.out.println("Checkbox selected");
    } else {
```

```
        System.out.println("Checkbox deselected");

    }

});
```

These controls allow users to interact with the application, and each component can have an event handler to respond to user actions.

9.5 Event Handling

Event handling in JavaFX allows applications to respond to user interactions. Events occur when users interact with controls, such as clicking buttons or typing in text fields.

Handling Button Click Events

To handle events, use the setOnAction method to assign an event handler to a control. For example:

java

```
Button button = new Button("Submit");

button.setOnAction(event ->
System.out.println("Button clicked!"));
```

In this case, the setOnAction method executes the code inside the lambda expression whenever the button is clicked.

9.6 Styling JavaFX Applications with CSS

JavaFX supports CSS for styling, allowing you to customize the appearance of UI components. CSS styles are added to a Scene or applied to individual components.

Basic CSS Styling Example

1. Create a CSS file (e.g., style.css):

css

```css
.button {
    -fx-background-color: #007acc;

    -fx-text-fill: white;

    -fx-font-size: 14px;
}
```

2. Load the CSS file in the JavaFX application:

java

```java
Scene scene = new Scene(vbox, 300, 200);

scene.getStylesheets().add("style.css");
```

This CSS applies a custom background color, text color, and font size to all buttons in the scene.

9.7 Creating a JavaFX Project: Simple Calculator

To apply the concepts learned in this chapter, we'll build a simple calculator with JavaFX that performs basic arithmetic operations.

Project Requirements

1. **Basic Arithmetic Operations**: Support addition, subtraction, multiplication, and division.

2. **User Interface**: Display buttons for numbers and operations, and show the result.

3. **Event Handling**: Process user inputs and display results.

Step 1: Define the Calculator Layout

java

```java
import javafx.application.Application;
import javafx.geometry.Insets;
import javafx.scene.Scene;
```

```java
import javafx.scene.control.Button;
import javafx.scene.control.TextField;
import javafx.scene.layout.GridPane;
import javafx.stage.Stage;

public class CalculatorApp extends Application {
    private TextField display = new TextField();

    @Override
    public void start(Stage primaryStage) {
        display.setEditable(false);
        display.setPrefSize(200, 50);

        GridPane gridPane = createLayout();
        Scene scene = new Scene(gridPane, 300, 400);

        primaryStage.setTitle("Calculator");
        primaryStage.setScene(scene);
        primaryStage.show();
    }
```

```java
private GridPane createLayout() {

    GridPane gridPane = new GridPane();

    gridPane.setPadding(new Insets(10));

    gridPane.setHgap(10);

    gridPane.setVgap(10);


    String[] buttons = {
        "7", "8", "9", "/",
        "4", "5", "6", "*",
        "1", "2", "3", "-",
        "0", ".", "=", "+"
    };


    int row = 1;
    int col = 0;
    for (String text : buttons) {

        Button button = new Button(text);

        button.setPrefSize(50, 50);

        gridPane.add(button, col, row);

        button.setOnAction(event ->
handleButtonClick(text));
```

```java
                col++;
                if (col == 4) {
                    col = 0;
                    row++;
                }
            }


        gridPane.add(display, 0, 0, 4, 1); // Display spans
4 columns
        return gridPane;
    }


    private void handleButtonClick(String text) {
        // Event handling logic will go here
    }


    public static void main(String[] args) {
        launch(args);
    }
}
```

In this setup:

- **GridPane**: Used to arrange buttons in a grid layout.

- **Button Array**: Represents calculator buttons, with each button assigned a label.

- **Event Handler**: handleButtonClick() processes button clicks.

Step 2: Implement Calculator Logic

Now, let's add basic calculator functionality by updating the handleButtonClick method.

java

```java
private double firstNumber = 0;

private String operator = "";

private boolean start = true;


private void handleButtonClick(String text) {
    if (text.matches("[0-9]") || text.equals(".")) {
        if (start) {
            display.clear();
            start = false;
        }
```

```java
        display.appendText(text);
    } else if (text.matches("[+\\-*/]")) {
        operator = text;
        firstNumber =
Double.parseDouble(display.getText());
        display.clear();
    } else if (text.equals("=")) {
        double secondNumber =
Double.parseDouble(display.getText());
        double result = calculateResult(firstNumber,
secondNumber, operator);
        display.setText(String.valueOf(result));
        start = true;
    }
}


private double calculateResult(double firstNumber,
double secondNumber, String operator) {
    return switch (operator) {
        case "+" -> firstNumber + secondNumber;
        case "-" -> firstNumber - secondNumber;
        case "*" -> firstNumber * secondNumber;
```

```
    case "/" -> secondNumber != 0 ? firstNumber /
secondNumber : 0;

    default -> 0;

  };

}
```

Explanation:

- **Number Input**: Appends digits or a decimal point to the display.

- **Operator Input**: Stores the current number and operator.

- **Calculate Result**: Computes the result when = is pressed and displays it.

Step 3: Style the Calculator

Add custom styling with CSS for a better user experience.

1. Create calculator.css:

css

```
.text-field {

  -fx-font-size: 20px;

  -fx-text-alignment: right;

}
```

```
.button {

    -fx-font-size: 18px;

    -fx-background-color: #007acc;

    -fx-text-fill: white;

}
```

2. Apply CSS to the scene:

java

```
scene.getStylesheets().add("calculator.css");
```

Conclusion

In this chapter, you learned the basics of GUI development with JavaFX, including layout management, event handling, and styling with CSS. We applied these concepts to build a simple calculator application, demonstrating the versatility and ease of use of JavaFX for creating graphical interfaces.

In the next chapter, we'll explore database connectivity with JDBC, allowing your applications to interact with databases and manage data persistently.

Chapter 10: Database Connectivity with JDBC

Introduction to JDBC

JDBC (Java Database Connectivity) is Java's standard API for connecting to relational databases. It provides a common interface for accessing different database management systems (DBMS), such as MySQL, PostgreSQL, and SQLite, allowing Java applications to interact with databases in a consistent way. Using JDBC, you can perform basic database operations like **CRUD** (Create, Read, Update, Delete) and manage data efficiently.

In this chapter, we'll explore JDBC's core components, learn how to execute SQL commands from Java, and implement a practical project that integrates database functionality.

10.1 Setting Up JDBC

Step 1: Install a Database

To work with JDBC, you'll need a database. For this example, we'll use MySQL, but the instructions can be adapted for other databases like PostgreSQL or SQLite.

1. Download and install MySQL Community Server.

2. Start the MySQL server and create a test database with user privileges.

Step 2: Add the JDBC Driver

To connect Java with MySQL, download the MySQL JDBC driver (MySQL Connector/J) from MySQL's website. Add the mysql-connector-java.jar file to your project's classpath.

In IntelliJ IDEA, go to **File > Project Structure > Libraries** and add the .jar file.

10.2 JDBC Architecture and Components

The JDBC API consists of several core components:

1. **DriverManager**: Manages a list of database drivers, handling connections based on the database URL.

2. **Connection**: Represents a session with the database.

3. **Statement**: Used to execute SQL queries.

4. **ResultSet**: Represents the result of an SQL query.

5. **PreparedStatement**: A subclass of Statement that supports parameterized queries, preventing SQL injection attacks.

These components work together to establish a connection, execute SQL queries, and process the results.

10.3 Connecting to a Database

To establish a connection, use the DriverManager.getConnection() method. The database URL format typically looks like this:

plaintext

jdbc:mysql://hostname:port/databaseName

Connecting to MySQL Example

```java
import java.sql.Connection;
import java.sql.DriverManager;
import java.sql.SQLException;

public class DatabaseConnection {
    private static final String URL = "jdbc:mysql://localhost:3306/testdb";
    private static final String USER = "root";
    private static final String PASSWORD = "password";

    public static Connection connect() {
        try {
            Connection connection = DriverManager.getConnection(URL, USER, PASSWORD);
            System.out.println("Connected to the database.");
            return connection;
        } catch (SQLException e) {
```

```java
            e.printStackTrace();

            return null;

        }

    }

}
```

In this code:

- URL specifies the database's location.

- USER and PASSWORD are the credentials for database access.

- DriverManager.getConnection() establishes the connection, which can then be used to interact with the database.

10.4 Executing SQL Queries with Statement

The Statement interface allows you to execute SQL queries, such as SELECT, INSERT, UPDATE, and DELETE.

Executing a SELECT Query

A SELECT query retrieves data from a database and stores it in a ResultSet object.

java

```java
import java.sql.Connection;

import java.sql.ResultSet;

import java.sql.SQLException;

import java.sql.Statement;


public class SelectExample {
    public static void main(String[] args) {

        try (Connection connection = DatabaseConnection.connect();

             Statement statement = connection.createStatement()) {


            String sql = "SELECT * FROM students";

            ResultSet resultSet = statement.executeQuery(sql);


            while (resultSet.next()) {
                int id = resultSet.getInt("id");
                String name = resultSet.getString("name");
                int age = resultSet.getInt("age");
```

```java
        System.out.println("ID: " + id + ", Name: " +
name + ", Age: " + age);

        }

    } catch (SQLException e) {

        e.printStackTrace();

    }

  }

}
```

This example executes a SELECT query and iterates over the results, displaying each student's details.

Executing an INSERT Query

An INSERT query adds new records to the database. Use executeUpdate() for INSERT, UPDATE, and DELETE operations as they modify the database.

java

```java
public class InsertExample {

  public static void main(String[] args) {

    try (Connection connection =
DatabaseConnection.connect();
```

```java
        Statement statement =
connection.createStatement()) {


        String sql = "INSERT INTO students (name,
age) VALUES ('John Doe', 22)";

        int rowsInserted =
statement.executeUpdate(sql);

        System.out.println("Rows inserted: " +
rowsInserted);

    } catch (SQLException e) {

        e.printStackTrace();

    }

  }

}
```

This code inserts a new student into the students table
and outputs the number of rows inserted.

10.5 Using PreparedStatement for Parameterized Queries

The PreparedStatement interface allows for
parameterized queries, which are both safer and more
efficient. It prevents SQL injection by separating SQL
logic from user input.

Using PreparedStatement for a SELECT Query

java

```java
import java.sql.Connection;

import java.sql.PreparedStatement;

import java.sql.ResultSet;

import java.sql.SQLException;


public class PreparedSelectExample {
    public static void main(String[] args) {
        String sql = "SELECT * FROM students WHERE age > ?";


        try (Connection connection = DatabaseConnection.connect();

             PreparedStatement preparedStatement = connection.prepareStatement(sql)) {


            preparedStatement.setInt(1, 18); // Set parameter for age
            ResultSet resultSet = preparedStatement.executeQuery();
```

```java
            while (resultSet.next()) {

                int id = resultSet.getInt("id");

                String name = resultSet.getString("name");

                int age = resultSet.getInt("age");

                System.out.println("ID: " + id + ", Name: " +
name + ", Age: " + age);

            }

        } catch (SQLException e) {

            e.printStackTrace();

        }

    }

}
```

Using PreparedStatement for an INSERT Query

java

```java
public class PreparedInsertExample {

    public static void main(String[] args) {

        String sql = "INSERT INTO students (name, age)
VALUES (?, ?)";
```

```java
    try (Connection connection =
DatabaseConnection.connect();

        PreparedStatement preparedStatement =
connection.prepareStatement(sql)) {


        preparedStatement.setString(1, "Jane Doe");

        preparedStatement.setInt(2, 20);

        int rowsInserted =
preparedStatement.executeUpdate();

        System.out.println("Rows inserted: " +
rowsInserted);

    } catch (SQLException e) {

        e.printStackTrace();

    }

    }

}
```

With PreparedStatement, you can reuse the same SQL query template with different parameters, making it more efficient for repeated queries.

10.6 Handling Transactions

Transactions are sequences of operations that are executed as a single unit. JDBC allows you to manage transactions to ensure data consistency, enabling **commit** and **rollback** operations.

Using Transactions in JDBC

java

```java
public class TransactionExample {

    public static void main(String[] args) {

        try (Connection connection =
DatabaseConnection.connect()) {

            connection.setAutoCommit(false); // Begin
transaction


            try (Statement statement =
connection.createStatement()) {

                statement.executeUpdate("INSERT INTO
students (name, age) VALUES ('Alice', 21)");
```

```
                statement.executeUpdate("UPDATE
students SET age = 22 WHERE name = 'Alice'");


                connection.commit(); // Commit transaction
                System.out.println("Transaction
committed.");
        } catch (SQLException e) {
                connection.rollback(); // Rollback if there's
an error
                System.out.println("Transaction rolled
back.");
                e.printStackTrace();

        }
    } catch (SQLException e) {
        e.printStackTrace();

    }
  }
}
```

In this example:

- **setAutoCommit(false)** begins the transaction.

- **commit()** confirms the transaction, applying changes.

- **rollback()** undoes changes if an error occurs.

10.7 Project: Student Management System

To apply the concepts in this chapter, we'll build a simple Student Management System with JDBC, allowing users to add, view, update, and delete student records in a MySQL database.

Step 1: Database Setup

Create a students table in your MySQL database:

sql

```sql
CREATE TABLE students (
    id INT AUTO_INCREMENT PRIMARY KEY,
    name VARCHAR(50) NOT NULL,
    age INT NOT NULL
);
```

Step 2: StudentManager Class

This class provides CRUD methods for managing students.

java

```java
import java.sql.Connection;

import java.sql.PreparedStatement;

import java.sql.ResultSet;

import java.sql.SQLException;


public class StudentManager {

    private Connection connection;


    public StudentManager(Connection connection) {

        this.connection = connection;

    }


    public void addStudent(String name, int age) throws
SQLException {

        String sql = "INSERT INTO students (name, age)
VALUES (?, ?)";

        try (PreparedStatement statement =
connection.prepareStatement(sql)) {

            statement.setString(1, name);

            statement.setInt(2, age);

            statement.executeUpdate();
```

```java
            System.out.println("Student added.");

        }

    }


    public void viewStudents() throws SQLException {

        String sql = "SELECT * FROM students";

        try (PreparedStatement statement =
connection.prepareStatement(sql)) {

            ResultSet resultSet =
statement.executeQuery();

            while (resultSet.next()) {

                int id = resultSet.getInt("id");

                String name = resultSet.getString("name");

                int age = resultSet.getInt("age");

                System.out.println("ID: " + id + ", Name: " +
name + ", Age: " + age);

            }

        }

    }


    public void updateStudent(int id, String name, int
age) throws SQLException {
```

```java
        String sql = "UPDATE students SET name = ?,
age = ? WHERE id = ?";

        try (PreparedStatement statement =
connection.prepareStatement(sql)) {

            statement.setString(1, name);

            statement.setInt(2, age);

            statement.setInt(3, id);

            statement.executeUpdate();

            System.out.println("Student updated.");

        }

    }


    public void deleteStudent(int id) throws
SQLException {

        String sql = "DELETE FROM students WHERE
id = ?";

        try (PreparedStatement statement =
connection.prepareStatement(sql)) {

            statement.setInt(1, id);

            statement.executeUpdate();

            System.out.println("Student deleted.");

        }
```

```
        }
}
```

Step 3: Main Class for User Interaction

The main class provides a simple console interface to interact with the StudentManager.

java

```java
import java.sql.Connection;
import java.sql.SQLException;
import java.util.Scanner;

public class Main {
    public static void main(String[] args) {
        try (Connection connection =
DatabaseConnection.connect()) {
            StudentManager manager = new
StudentManager(connection);
            Scanner scanner = new Scanner(System.in);

            while (true) {
                System.out.println("\n1. Add Student");
                System.out.println("2. View Students");
```

```java
System.out.println("3. Update Student");
System.out.println("4. Delete Student");
System.out.println("5. Exit");
System.out.print("Choose an option: ");
int choice = scanner.nextInt();

switch (choice) {
    case 1:
        System.out.print("Enter name: ");
        String name = scanner.next();
        System.out.print("Enter age: ");
        int age = scanner.nextInt();
        manager.addStudent(name, age);
        break;
    case 2:
        manager.viewStudents();
        break;
    case 3:
        System.out.print("Enter student ID to update: ");
        int updateId = scanner.nextInt();
```

```java
                System.out.print("Enter new name: ");

                String newName = scanner.next();

                System.out.print("Enter new age: ");

                int newAge = scanner.nextInt();

                manager.updateStudent(updateId,
newName, newAge);

                break;
            case 4:

                System.out.print("Enter student ID to
delete: ");

                int deleteId = scanner.nextInt();

                manager.deleteStudent(deleteId);

                break;
            case 5:

                System.out.println("Exiting...");

                scanner.close();

                return;
            default:

                System.out.println("Invalid option.");

                break;

        }
```

```
        }

    } catch (SQLException e) {

        e.printStackTrace();

    }

  }

}
```

This code provides a simple text-based interface, allowing users to add, view, update, and delete student records. Each action is mapped to a corresponding method in the StudentManager class, demonstrating the use of JDBC for CRUD operations.

Conclusion

In this chapter, you learned the essentials of JDBC, from establishing database connections to executing SQL queries and handling transactions. We also built a Student Management System that demonstrates how to apply these skills in a real-world application. With JDBC, Java applications can manage data stored in relational databases, enabling you to build data-driven applications efficiently.

In the next chapter, we'll explore deploying Java applications, ensuring your software can be distributed and run on various platforms effectively.

Chapter 11: Building and Deploying Java Applications

Introduction to Building and Deployment

Developing software doesn't stop at writing code; building and deployment are crucial steps in making your application accessible to users. In Java, this process involves compiling code, managing dependencies, packaging the application, and distributing it. Java provides several tools to streamline these tasks, including the Java Development Kit (JDK), build tools like Maven and Gradle, and deployment solutions that make applications available on various platforms.

In this chapter, we'll focus on building Java applications and explore deployment options to make your application ready for end-users.

11.1 Packaging Java Applications with JAR Files

A **Java Archive (JAR) file** is a compressed file format that bundles Java classes, resources, and metadata into a single, executable package. JAR files make it easy to distribute Java applications since all necessary files are packaged together.

Creating an Executable JAR File

An executable JAR file contains a Main-Class entry in its manifest, allowing the JAR to be run from the command line with a simple command.

1. **Compile the Application**:

Compile your application's Java files into bytecode using the javac command.

bash

```
javac -d out src/*.java
```

2. **Create the JAR File**:

Use the jar command to package your application. Specify the entry point (the class with the main method) in the -e option.

bash

```
jar cfe MyApplication.jar MainClass -C out .
```

3. **Run the JAR File**:

You can execute the JAR file using the java -jar command.

bash

```
java -jar MyApplication.jar
```

An executable JAR file is ideal for deploying standalone desktop applications, as it includes all compiled classes and resources.

11.2 Managing Dependencies with Build Tools

Java applications often depend on external libraries. Manually managing these libraries can become complex, especially for large projects. Build tools like **Maven** and **Gradle** simplify dependency management, automate the build process, and streamline tasks like compiling code, running tests, and packaging the application.

Using Maven

Apache Maven is a popular build tool that uses a pom.xml file to manage dependencies, configure plugins, and define project structure.

1. **Set Up Maven Project**:

Initialize a Maven project with the following directory structure:

css

MyProject
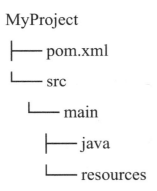
├── pom.xml
└── src
    └── main
        ├── java
        └── resources

2. **Define Dependencies**:

In the pom.xml file, add dependencies in the <dependencies> section. For example, if your project requires the Gson library, add it as follows:

xml

```
<dependencies>
  <dependency>
    <groupId>com.google.code.gson</groupId>
    <artifactId>gson</artifactId>
    <version>2.8.8</version>
```

```
</dependency>
```

```
</dependencies>
```

3. **Build and Package**:

Use Maven commands to compile, test, and package your application.

bash

```
mvn clean compile      # Compile source files

mvn test            # Run tests

mvn package            # Create a JAR file in the target/
directory
```

Maven simplifies dependency management by automatically downloading required libraries and ensuring your project is up to date.

Using Gradle

Gradle is a versatile build tool that uses a Groovy or Kotlin DSL to configure projects. It's popular for large, complex applications due to its flexibility.

1. **Set Up Gradle Project**:

Initialize a Gradle project using the following directory structure:

css

```
MyProject
├── build.gradle
└── src
    └── main
        ├── java
        └── resources
```

2. Define Dependencies:

In the build.gradle file, add dependencies in the dependencies block. For example:

groovy

```groovy
dependencies {
    implementation 'com.google.code.gson:gson:2.8.8'
}
```

3. Build and Package:

Use Gradle commands to compile, test, and package your application.

bash

```bash
gradle build   # Builds and tests the application,
creating a JAR file in build/libs/
```

Gradle's powerful configuration capabilities make it suitable for large-scale projects, supporting complex dependency management and advanced build logic.

11.3 Creating a Distribution

Creating a distribution package involves more than just bundling JAR files; it requires including configuration files, dependencies, and instructions for end-users.

Distribution Structure

A typical distribution package includes:

- **Executable JAR**: The main application.

- **Lib Folder**: Additional dependencies.

- **Config Folder**: Configuration files.

- **ReadMe File**: Instructions for users.

Example directory structure:

arduino

MyApp
├── MyApplication.jar
├── lib
│   └── gson-2.8.8.jar

```
├── config
│   └── app.properties
└── README.txt
```

This layout makes it easy for users to understand where resources are located and what dependencies are required.

11.4 Deploying Desktop Applications

Java desktop applications can be deployed as JAR files, Java Web Start applications, or native executables using tools like **jpackage**.

Creating a Native Installer with jpackage

The jpackage tool, introduced in JDK 14, packages Java applications into platform-specific installers (e.g., .exe for Windows, .dmg for macOS).

bash

```bash
jpackage --input out --name MyApp --main-jar MyApplication.jar --type dmg
```

This command creates a macOS .dmg installer, making it easier for users to install the application. jpackage supports multiple formats, including .exe for Windows and .deb for Linux.

11.5 Deploying Web Applications

Web applications built with Java typically use frameworks like **Spring** or **Java EE** and are packaged as **WAR** files for deployment on a web server or servlet container.

Creating a WAR File

A **Web Application Archive (WAR)** file packages Java web applications, including all resources, classes, and configuration files.

1. **Set Up a Web Application**:

Create a typical web application directory structure:

css

```
MyWebApp
├── src
├── web
│   ├── WEB-INF
│   │   ├── web.xml
│   │   └── classes
└── pom.xml
```

2. **Build and Package the WAR**:

Use Maven to package the application as a WAR file:

bash

mvn package

The generated WAR file is located in the target/ directory.

3. **Deploy to a Server**:

Deploy the WAR file to a servlet container like **Apache Tomcat** by placing it in the webapps directory. Tomcat automatically deploys the WAR, making the application accessible via a URL.

11.6 Continuous Integration and Deployment (CI/CD)

Continuous Integration (CI) and Continuous Deployment (CD) are practices that automate building, testing, and deploying applications. Tools like **Jenkins, GitLab CI**, and **GitHub Actions** allow you to automate these tasks.

Setting Up Jenkins for CI/CD

1. **Install Jenkins**:

Download and install Jenkins from jenkins.io.

2. **Configure a Pipeline**:

Create a Jenkins pipeline to automate build, test, and deployment tasks. For example, a Jenkinsfile might look like this:

groovy

```groovy
pipeline {
    agent any
    stages {
        stage('Build') {
            steps {
                sh 'mvn clean compile'
            }
        }
        stage('Test') {
            steps {
                sh 'mvn test'
            }
        }
        stage('Package') {
```

```
        steps {

            sh 'mvn package'

        }

    }

    stage('Deploy') {

        steps {

            sh 'scp target/MyApp.jar
user@server:/path/to/deploy'

        }

    }

  }

}
```

This pipeline compiles, tests, packages, and deploys the application to a remote server. Jenkins can be configured to run this pipeline automatically upon code changes, streamlining the development and deployment process.

11.7 Deployment on Cloud Platforms

Cloud platforms like **AWS**, **Google Cloud**, and **Azure** offer scalable environments to host Java applications, making it easy to deploy web services or backend systems.

Deploying to AWS Elastic Beanstalk

1. **Create a WAR File**:

Package your Java web application as a WAR file.

2. **Deploy to Elastic Beanstalk**:

Log in to the AWS Management Console and create an Elastic Beanstalk environment, specifying **Java** as the platform.

3. **Upload the WAR File**:

Upload the WAR file to Elastic Beanstalk, and AWS handles provisioning, scaling, and managing the environment for you.

Elastic Beanstalk provides automatic scaling and load balancing, making it ideal for Java applications that need high availability.

Deploying to Heroku

Heroku simplifies Java application deployment by abstracting server management and scaling.

1. **Install the Heroku CLI** and log in to your account.

bash

```
heroku login
```

2. **Initialize and Deploy**:

bash

heroku create

git push heroku main

3. **Access the Application**:

Once deployed, Heroku assigns a URL to access your application.

Heroku's one-click deployment and automatic scaling make it ideal for quick, scalable deployments.

11.8 Project: Deploying a Java Web Application

To demonstrate deployment, we'll create a simple web application that displays a welcome message and deploy it to a Tomcat server.

Step 1: Web Application Structure

Set up a basic project structure:

css

MyWebApp

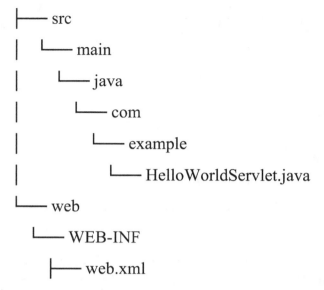

```
├── src
│    └── main
│         └── java
│              └── com
│                   └── example
│                        └── HelloWorldServlet.java
└── web
     └── WEB-INF
          ├── web.xml
```

Step 2: Create the HelloWorldServlet

java

package com.example;

import java.io.IOException;

import javax.servlet.ServletException;

import javax.servlet.http.HttpServlet;

import javax.servlet.http.HttpServletRequest;

import javax.servlet.http.HttpServletResponse;

public class HelloWorldServlet extends HttpServlet {

```java
@Override
protected void doGet(HttpServletRequest request,
HttpServletResponse response)
    throws ServletException, IOException {
    response.setContentType("text/html");
    response.getWriter().println("<h1>Hello, World
from Java Web App!</h1>");
    }
}
```

Step 3: Configure web.xml

xml

```xml
<web-app>
  <servlet>
    <servlet-name>HelloWorldServlet</servlet-
name>
    <servlet-
class>com.example.HelloWorldServlet</servlet-class>
  </servlet>
  <servlet-mapping>
    <servlet-name>HelloWorldServlet</servlet-
name>
```

```
<url-pattern>/hello</url-pattern>

</servlet-mapping>
```

```
</web-app>
```

Step 4: Build and Deploy

1. Package the application as a WAR file using Maven or manually.

2. Place the WAR file in Tomcat's webapps directory and start the Tomcat server.

3. Access the application at http://localhost:8080/MyWebApp/hello.

This project demonstrates the process of deploying a simple Java web application on a servlet container, providing a foundation for more complex deployments.

Conclusion

In this chapter, we explored the steps involved in building and deploying Java applications. We covered creating JAR files, managing dependencies with Maven and Gradle, and deploying applications on desktop, web, and cloud platforms. By understanding the build and deployment process, you're equipped to make your Java applications accessible to users on various platforms.

In the next chapter, we'll cover advanced Java topics like reflection and annotations, enabling you to develop more flexible and dynamic applications.

Chapter 12: Final Project – Real-World Java Application

Project Overview

For this final project, we'll build a **Personal Finance Manager**, a desktop application that helps users track their income, expenses, and budgets. The application will include the following features:

1. **User Interface**: A JavaFX-based GUI for user interactions.

2. **Database**: Persistent storage using MySQL and JDBC for storing income and expense data.

3. **Multithreading**: Background tasks for data processing to keep the interface responsive.

4. **Reporting**: Generate reports on monthly and yearly spending.

5. **Deployment**: Package the application for easy distribution.

12.1 Application Architecture and Design

Main Components

1. **Database Layer**: Manages data persistence using JDBC with a MySQL database.

2. **Service Layer**: Contains the business logic, including calculations and processing.

3. **User Interface Layer**: Provides a JavaFX-based GUI for user interactions.

4. **Controller Layer**: Handles user input, interfaces between the UI and service layers, and manages multi-threaded operations.

12.2 Setting Up the Database

Database Schema

Create a finance_db database with two main tables: income and expenses.

sql

```
CREATE DATABASE finance_db;
```

```sql
USE finance_db;

CREATE TABLE income (
    id INT AUTO_INCREMENT PRIMARY KEY,
    date DATE NOT NULL,
    category VARCHAR(50),
    amount DECIMAL(10, 2) NOT NULL
);

CREATE TABLE expenses (
    id INT AUTO_INCREMENT PRIMARY KEY,
    date DATE NOT NULL,
    category VARCHAR(50),
    amount DECIMAL(10, 2) NOT NULL
);
```

These tables store the date, category, and amount for each income and expense entry. You'll need to configure your MySQL user credentials in the application's database connection class.

12.3 Database Connectivity with JDBC

Create a DatabaseConnection class that handles database connections.

java

```java
import java.sql.Connection;

import java.sql.DriverManager;

import java.sql.SQLException;


public class DatabaseConnection {

    private static final String URL =
"jdbc:mysql://localhost:3306/finance_db";

    private static final String USER = "root";

    private static final String PASSWORD =
"password";


    public static Connection connect() {

        try {

            return DriverManager.getConnection(URL,
USER, PASSWORD);

        } catch (SQLException e) {
```

```
        e.printStackTrace();

        return null;

    }

  }

}
```

12.4 Service Layer for Business Logic

The service layer contains classes that handle business logic, such as adding, updating, and retrieving income and expense records.

IncomeService Class

java

```
import java.sql.Connection;

import java.sql.PreparedStatement;

import java.sql.ResultSet;

import java.sql.SQLException;

import java.util.ArrayList;

import java.util.List;
```

```java
public class IncomeService {

  public void addIncome(String category, double
amount) {

    String sql = "INSERT INTO income (date,
category, amount) VALUES (CURDATE(), ?, ?)";

    try (Connection connection =
DatabaseConnection.connect();

       PreparedStatement statement =
connection.prepareStatement(sql)) {

       statement.setString(1, category);

       statement.setDouble(2, amount);

       statement.executeUpdate();

    } catch (SQLException e) {

       e.printStackTrace();

    }

  }


  public List<String> getIncomeReport() {

    List<String> report = new ArrayList<>();

    String sql = "SELECT * FROM income ORDER
BY date";

    try (Connection connection =
DatabaseConnection.connect();
```

```java
        PreparedStatement statement =
connection.prepareStatement(sql);

        ResultSet resultSet =
statement.executeQuery()) {

        while (resultSet.next()) {

        String entry = "Date: " +
resultSet.getDate("date") + ", Category: " +

                resultSet.getString("category") + ",
Amount: $" + resultSet.getDouble("amount");

        report.add(entry);

        }

    } catch (SQLException e) {

        e.printStackTrace();

    }

    return report;

  }

}
```

12.5 Building the JavaFX GUI

The JavaFX GUI provides an intuitive interface for adding income and expenses, viewing reports, and managing finances.

Main Layout

The main layout will include tabs for **Income**, **Expenses**, and **Reports**. Each tab will contain a form for adding entries and a table for viewing records.

Building the GUI

1. **Create a Main Application Window**:

java

```
import javafx.application.Application;

import javafx.scene.Scene;

import javafx.scene.control.Tab;

import javafx.scene.control.TabPane;

import javafx.stage.Stage;


public class FinanceManagerApp extends Application
{
    @Override
    public void start(Stage primaryStage) {
        TabPane tabPane = new TabPane();
        tabPane.getTabs().addAll(
            createIncomeTab(),
            createExpensesTab(),
```

```java
        createReportTab()
    );


    Scene scene = new Scene(tabPane, 600, 400);
    primaryStage.setTitle("Personal Finance
Manager");
    primaryStage.setScene(scene);
    primaryStage.show();
}


private Tab createIncomeTab() {
    Tab incomeTab = new Tab("Income");
    incomeTab.setContent(new
IncomeTab().getContent());
    return incomeTab;
}


private Tab createExpensesTab() {
    Tab expensesTab = new Tab("Expenses");
    expensesTab.setContent(new
ExpensesTab().getContent());
    return expensesTab;
```

```
    }


    private Tab createReportTab() {

        Tab reportTab = new Tab("Reports");

        reportTab.setContent(new
ReportTab().getContent());

        return reportTab;

    }


    public static void main(String[] args) {

        launch(args);

    }

}
```

2. **Implement the Income Tab**

java

```java
import javafx.geometry.Insets;

import javafx.scene.control.Button;

import javafx.scene.control.Label;

import javafx.scene.control.TextField;

import javafx.scene.layout.GridPane;
```

```java
public class IncomeTab {

    private IncomeService incomeService = new
IncomeService();

    public GridPane getContent() {
        GridPane grid = new GridPane();
        grid.setPadding(new Insets(10));
        grid.setHgap(10);
        grid.setVgap(10);

        Label categoryLabel = new Label("Category:");
        TextField categoryField = new TextField();
        Label amountLabel = new Label("Amount:");
        TextField amountField = new TextField();

        Button addButton = new Button("Add Income");
        addButton.setOnAction(e -> {
            String category = categoryField.getText();
            double amount =
Double.parseDouble(amountField.getText());
```

```java
        incomeService.addIncome(category, amount);

        categoryField.clear();

        amountField.clear();

    });


    grid.add(categoryLabel, 0, 0);

    grid.add(categoryField, 1, 0);

    grid.add(amountLabel, 0, 1);

    grid.add(amountField, 1, 1);

    grid.add(addButton, 1, 2);


    return grid;

  }

}
```

3. **Implement the Report Tab**

java

```java
import javafx.scene.control.TextArea;

import javafx.scene.layout.VBox;


public class ReportTab {
```

```java
    private IncomeService incomeService = new
IncomeService();


    public VBox getContent() {

        VBox vbox = new VBox(10);

        TextArea reportArea = new TextArea();

        reportArea.setEditable(false);


        reportArea.setText(String.join("\n",
incomeService.getIncomeReport()));


        vbox.getChildren().add(reportArea);

        return vbox;

    }

}
```

This setup provides a basic UI for managing income records. Repeat similar steps to create the Expenses tab and integrate its functionality.

12.6 Multithreading for a Responsive UI

Long-running database operations can freeze the GUI. Use JavaFX's Task class to run these operations in the background, keeping the interface responsive.

java

```java
import javafx.concurrent.Task;


public void
fetchIncomeReportInBackground(TextArea
reportArea) {

    Task<List<String>> task = new Task<>() {

        @Override

        protected List<String> call() {

            return incomeService.getIncomeReport();

        }

    };


    task.setOnSucceeded(e ->
reportArea.setText(String.join("\n", task.getValue())));

    new Thread(task).start();
```

}

This code fetches income data on a separate thread and updates the GUI once the task completes.

12.7 Packaging and Deploying the Application

1. Package as an Executable JAR:

Use Maven or Gradle to package the application as an executable JAR with dependencies included.

2. Create a Distribution Folder:

Include the JAR, a README file, and a config folder (for database configurations) in the distribution package.

3. Using jpackage for Installer:

Create a platform-specific installer using jpackage:

bash

```
jpackage --input out --name FinanceManager --main-jar FinanceManagerApp.jar --type exe
```

This command packages the application as an .exe for Windows. Replace exe with dmg for macOS or deb for Linux.

12.8 Testing and Finalizing the Application

1. **Test Database Operations**:

Verify that all database operations work as expected, ensuring accurate addition, updating, and retrieval of records.

2. **UI Testing**:

Test each GUI component, validating that inputs are handled correctly and error messages display for invalid inputs.

3. **Final Deployment**:

Deploy the application package to your desired platform and test installation on different machines.

Conclusion

In this final project, you built a complete, real-world Java application from scratch. You applied concepts like database connectivity, GUI development with JavaFX, multithreading, and deployment to create a Personal Finance Manager. This project demonstrates how all the skills and tools you've learned come together in a cohesive, functional application, giving you the foundation to develop more complex and professional Java applications.

With this project, you've successfully completed a comprehensive journey through Java development. You're now equipped to tackle real-world programming challenges and explore even more advanced topics in Java development.

Chapter 13: Unit Testing and Test-Driven Development (TDD) in Java

Introduction to Unit Testing

Unit testing involves testing individual components or "units" of code, typically at the method level, to ensure they perform correctly. Unit tests are isolated from the rest of the application, allowing developers to test functionality in a controlled environment without interference from other parts of the codebase. Well-written unit tests make code easier to maintain, reduce the likelihood of bugs, and provide confidence when making changes.

Unit testing is critical in larger applications where multiple components interact; by catching errors early, you can prevent costly debugging and rewrites later on.

13.1 Benefits of Unit Testing

1. **Early Bug Detection**: Unit tests help identify errors early in the development cycle.

2. **Code Stability**: With unit tests, refactoring becomes safer, as you can quickly confirm that functionality remains intact.

3. **Documentation**: Tests serve as a form of documentation, showing how methods are intended to be used.

4. **Code Modularity**: Writing unit tests encourages modular code design, which improves code readability and maintainability.

13.2 Introduction to JUnit Framework

JUnit is a popular testing framework in Java that simplifies the process of writing and running unit tests. JUnit provides annotations for defining test methods, managing test setup, and running assertions to verify that code behaves as expected.

Setting Up JUnit

To start using JUnit, add it to your project dependencies. If using Maven, add the following to your pom.xml:

xml

```xml
<dependencies>

   <dependency>

      <groupId>org.junit.jupiter</groupId>

      <artifactId>junit-jupiter-engine</artifactId>

      <version>5.8.1</version>

      <scope>test</scope>

   </dependency>

</dependencies>
```

JUnit 5 is the latest version, and it includes junit-jupiter for writing tests and junit-platform for running them.

13.3 Writing Basic Unit Tests with JUnit

JUnit uses annotations to define test methods, setup methods, and teardown methods. Here's a quick overview:

- **@Test**: Marks a method as a test case.

- **@BeforeEach**: Executes setup code before each test.

- **@AfterEach**: Executes cleanup code after each test.

- **@BeforeAll** and **@AfterAll**: Execute setup/teardown once for all tests in the class.

Basic JUnit Test Example

java

```java
import org.junit.jupiter.api.BeforeEach;
import org.junit.jupiter.api.Test;
import static org.junit.jupiter.api.Assertions.*;

public class CalculatorTest {
    private Calculator calculator;

    @BeforeEach
    public void setUp() {
        calculator = new Calculator();
    }
```

```java
@Test
public void testAddition() {

    assertEquals(5, calculator.add(2, 3));

}


@Test
public void testSubtraction() {

    assertEquals(2, calculator.subtract(5, 3));

}
}
```

In this example:

- The CalculatorTest class contains test cases for the Calculator class.

- The setUp() method initializes the Calculator instance before each test.

- Each test method uses assertions (like assertEquals) to check that results match expectations.

13.4 Assertions in JUnit

Assertions are used to verify that test results are as expected. Commonly used assertions include:

- **assertEquals(expected, actual)**: Checks if two values are equal.

- **assertTrue(condition)**: Verifies that a condition is true.

- **assertFalse(condition)**: Verifies that a condition is false.

- **assertNull(value)**: Checks that a value is null.

- **assertNotNull(value)**: Checks that a value is not null.

- **assertThrows(Exception.class, () -> code)**: Verifies that an exception is thrown.

For example:

java

```java
@Test
public void testDivision() {
    assertThrows(ArithmeticException.class, () ->
    calculator.divide(10, 0));
}
```

In this test, assertThrows checks that an ArithmeticException is thrown when dividing by zero.

13.5 Writing Parameterized Tests

JUnit allows you to run the same test with multiple sets of parameters, which can be useful when you need to verify behavior across a range of inputs.

Using @ParameterizedTest

java

```java
import org.junit.jupiter.params.ParameterizedTest;
import org.junit.jupiter.params.provider.ValueSource;

public class CalculatorTest {
    @ParameterizedTest
    @ValueSource(ints = {1, 2, 3, 5, 8})
    public void testIsPositive(int number) {
        assertTrue(calculator.isPositive(number));
    }
}
```

In this test, @ValueSource provides multiple integer values, and the testIsPositive method is run once for each value. This is helpful for validating a method's behavior with different inputs.

13.6 Test-Driven Development (TDD)

Test-Driven Development (TDD) is a methodology where you write tests before implementing code. TDD follows a "red-green-refactor" cycle:

1. **Red**: Write a failing test that specifies the desired behavior.

2. **Green**: Write just enough code to make the test pass.

3. **Refactor**: Clean up the code, improving design and readability without changing functionality.

Benefits of TDD

- **Design-Driven**: TDD encourages you to think about how the code should behave before writing it.

- **Improved Code Quality**: Writing tests first often leads to more modular, testable code.

- **Documentation by Testing**: Tests written during TDD serve as a clear, up-to-date specification of code behavior.

13.7 TDD in Practice: A Step-by-Step Example

Let's walk through the TDD process by building a simple BankAccount class that supports deposit, withdraw, and balance-check functionalities.

Step 1: Write the First Test (Red)

First, write a test for a deposit method in BankAccount:

java

```java
import org.junit.jupiter.api.BeforeEach;

import org.junit.jupiter.api.Test;

import static org.junit.jupiter.api.Assertions.*;


public class BankAccountTest {

    private BankAccount account;


    @BeforeEach
    public void setUp() {

        account = new BankAccount(100); // Initial
balance of 100

    }
```

```java
@Test
public void testDeposit() {
    account.deposit(50);
    assertEquals(150, account.getBalance());
}
}
```

This test checks that after depositing $50, the account balance is $150. Since the deposit method doesn't exist yet, this test will fail.

Step 2: Implement the Code (Green)

Create a minimal BankAccount class that passes the test.

java

```java
public class BankAccount {
    private double balance;

    public BankAccount(double initialBalance) {
        this.balance = initialBalance;
    }
```

```java
public void deposit(double amount) {

    balance += amount;

}


public double getBalance() {

    return balance;

    }

}
```

The deposit method adds the given amount to the balance, making the test pass.

Step 3: Refactor

Examine the code and look for improvements. In this case, there may be nothing to refactor yet, but as the class grows, you'll likely identify opportunities to streamline and improve design.

Repeat for Withdraw Functionality

Next, add a test for the withdraw method.

java

```java
@Test
public void testWithdraw() {

    account.withdraw(30);
```

```
        assertEquals(70, account.getBalance());
}
```

Implement the withdraw method, ensuring it passes the test.

java

```java
public void withdraw(double amount) {
    if (amount <= balance) {
        balance -= amount;
    } else {
        throw new
IllegalArgumentException("Insufficient balance");
    }
}
```

Add a test to check that an exception is thrown for an overdraft.

java

```java
@Test
public void testWithdrawInsufficientFunds() {
    assertThrows(IllegalArgumentException.class, () ->
account.withdraw(200));
```

}

By following TDD, you continue writing tests and implementing code in small increments, ensuring that each method behaves as expected.

13.8 Mocking and Testing with External Dependencies

Some methods interact with external dependencies, like databases or web services, which can complicate unit testing. **Mocking** is a technique that allows you to simulate the behavior of these dependencies.

Using Mockito for Mocking

Mockito is a popular Java mocking framework that allows you to create mock objects and specify their behavior.

Add Mockito to your dependencies:

xml

```
<dependency>
    <groupId>org.mockito</groupId>
    <artifactId>mockito-core</artifactId>
    <version>3.11.2</version>
```

```
    <scope>test</scope>

</dependency>
```

Mocking Example

Let's say BankAccount has a DatabaseService dependency. Here's how to test methods that interact with the database using Mockito:

java

```java
import org.junit.jupiter.api.BeforeEach;

import org.junit.jupiter.api.Test;

import org.mockito.InjectMocks;

import org.mockito.Mock;

import org.mockito.MockitoAnnotations;


import static org.mockito.Mockito.*;

import static org.junit.jupiter.api.Assertions.*;


public class BankAccountTest {

    @Mock

    private DatabaseService databaseService;
```

```java
@InjectMocks
private BankAccount account;

@BeforeEach
public void setUp() {
    MockitoAnnotations.openMocks(this);
    account = new BankAccount(100);
}

@Test
public void testDepositUpdatesDatabase() {
    account.deposit(50);
    verify(databaseService).updateBalance(150);
}
}
```

- **@Mock**: Creates a mock object for DatabaseService.
- **@InjectMocks**: Injects the mock object into BankAccount.
- **verify()**: Confirms that the updateBalance method is called with the correct parameter.

Mocking enables you to test code with dependencies in isolation, making tests faster and more reliable.

13.9 Best Practices for Unit Testing and TDD

1. **Write Independent Tests**: Each test should run independently of others to avoid unintended side effects.

2. **Keep Tests Fast**: Unit tests should be quick, enabling frequent test runs and faster feedback.

3. **Use Meaningful Names**: Name your tests clearly to indicate what functionality they're verifying.

4. **Cover Edge Cases**: Test both typical and edge-case inputs to ensure robust functionality.

5. **Follow the "Arrange-Act-Assert" Pattern**:

   o **Arrange**: Set up necessary data or objects.

   o **Act**: Call the method under test.

   o **Assert**: Verify that the outcome is as expected.

13.10 Final Thoughts on TDD and Testing in Java

Test-Driven Development and unit testing are invaluable practices for creating high-quality software. By writing tests before code, TDD encourages thoughtful design and leads to more modular, reliable, and maintainable applications. With unit tests in place, you can refactor code with confidence, knowing that any issues will be quickly identified.

This chapter introduced you to the basics of unit testing with JUnit, explored parameterized testing, TDD practices, and advanced techniques like mocking with Mockito. As you continue developing Java applications, implementing these practices will enhance your software's stability, usability, and overall quality.

In the next chapter, we'll explore advanced topics in Java, such as reflection and annotations, to further extend the capabilities of your Java applications.

Chapter 14: Design Patterns in Java

Introduction to Design Patterns

A design pattern is a general, reusable solution to a common problem in software design. Patterns are not specific pieces of code but rather templates or strategies that can be adapted to fit various contexts. The concept of design patterns was popularized by the "Gang of Four" (GoF) book, which identified 23 patterns widely applicable across different programming languages, including Java.

Benefits of Using Design Patterns

1. **Standardized Solutions**: Patterns provide well-known, standardized approaches to solving common problems.

2. **Code Reusability**: By following patterns, code becomes easier to reuse across projects.

3. **Enhanced Collaboration**: Patterns create a shared vocabulary, making it easier to

communicate design decisions with other developers.

4. **Increased Flexibility**: Patterns often promote flexibility by decoupling components, making it easier to extend functionality.

14.1 Creational Patterns

Creational patterns focus on object creation mechanisms, aiming to reduce complexity and ensure objects are created in a controlled way.

Singleton Pattern

The **Singleton** pattern ensures that a class has only one instance and provides a global point of access to that instance. This pattern is useful when managing shared resources, such as database connections or configuration settings.

Implementation Example

java

```java
public class Singleton {
    private static Singleton instance;

    private Singleton() {
```

```java
        // private constructor to prevent instantiation
    }

    public static Singleton getInstance() {
        if (instance == null) {
            instance = new Singleton();
        }
        return instance;
    }
}
```

In this example:

- The constructor is private, preventing external instantiation.

- getInstance() checks if an instance exists; if not, it creates one.

Usage

java

```java
Singleton singleton = Singleton.getInstance();
```

The Singleton pattern ensures there is only one instance of the Singleton class, which is accessed globally.

Factory Method Pattern

The **Factory Method** pattern defines an interface for creating an object but allows subclasses to alter the type of object created. It's useful when the creation process varies based on input or context.

Implementation Example

java

```java
public abstract class Animal {
    public abstract String makeSound();
}


class Dog extends Animal {
    public String makeSound() {
        return "Woof!";
    }
}


class Cat extends Animal {
    public String makeSound() {
        return "Meow!";
    }
```

```java
}

class AnimalFactory {
    public static Animal createAnimal(String type) {
        switch (type.toLowerCase()) {
            case "dog": return new Dog();
            case "cat": return new Cat();
            default: throw new
IllegalArgumentException("Unknown animal type");
        }
    }
}
```

Usage

java

```java
Animal animal = AnimalFactory.createAnimal("dog");

System.out.println(animal.makeSound()); // Output:
Woof!
```

The Factory Method pattern encapsulates object creation, enabling the creation of different types of objects without directly using constructors.

14.2 Structural Patterns

Structural patterns deal with object composition and relationships, providing solutions for organizing classes and objects into larger structures.

Adapter Pattern

The **Adapter** pattern allows incompatible interfaces to work together by creating a wrapper class that adapts one interface to another. It's useful for integrating third-party libraries with different interfaces.

Implementation Example

java

```java
public interface MediaPlayer {
    void play(String audioType, String fileName);
}


class MP3Player implements MediaPlayer {
    public void play(String audioType, String fileName) {
        System.out.println("Playing MP3: " + fileName);
    }
}
```

```java
class MP4Player {
    public void playMp4(String fileName) {
        System.out.println("Playing MP4: " + fileName);
    }
}


class MediaAdapter implements MediaPlayer {
    private MP4Player mp4Player = new MP4Player();

    public void play(String audioType, String fileName) {
        if ("mp4".equalsIgnoreCase(audioType)) {
            mp4Player.playMp4(fileName);
        } else {
            System.out.println("Format not supported.");
        }
    }
}
```

Usage

java

MediaPlayer player = new MediaAdapter();

player.play("mp4", "video.mp4"); // Output: Playing
MP4: video.mp4

The Adapter pattern allows MediaPlayer to work with
MP4Player, even though their interfaces differ.

Decorator Pattern

The **Decorator** pattern adds functionality to an object
dynamically, without modifying its structure. This
pattern is ideal for enhancing or extending the
behavior of classes in a flexible and reusable way.

Implementation Example

java

```java
public interface Coffee {

    String getDescription();

    double getCost();

}


class SimpleCoffee implements Coffee {

    public String getDescription() {

        return "Simple coffee";
```

```java
        }

        public double getCost() {
            return 2.0;
        }
    }

    class MilkDecorator implements Coffee {
        private Coffee coffee;

        public MilkDecorator(Coffee coffee) {
            this.coffee = coffee;
        }

        public String getDescription() {
            return coffee.getDescription() + ", milk";
        }

        public double getCost() {
            return coffee.getCost() + 0.5;
        }
```

}

Usage

java

Coffee coffee = new MilkDecorator(new SimpleCoffee());

System.out.println(coffee.getDescription()); // Output: Simple coffee, milk

System.out.println(coffee.getCost()); // Output: 2.5

The Decorator pattern allows you to add new functionality (milk) to an object (SimpleCoffee) without modifying its structure.

14.3 Behavioral Patterns

Behavioral patterns focus on communication between objects, defining how they interact and distribute responsibility.

Observer Pattern

The **Observer** pattern allows objects (observers) to subscribe to events in another object (subject), receiving updates when the subject's state changes. This is useful in event-driven applications.

Implementation Example

```java
java

import java.util.ArrayList;
import java.util.List;

interface Observer {
    void update(String message);
}

class Subject {
    private List<Observer> observers = new
ArrayList<>();

    public void addObserver(Observer observer) {
        observers.add(observer);
    }

    public void notifyObservers(String message) {
        for (Observer observer : observers) {
            observer.update(message);
        }
```

```java
    }
}

class ConcreteObserver implements Observer {
    private String name;

    public ConcreteObserver(String name) {
        this.name = name;
    }

    public void update(String message) {
        System.out.println(name + " received update: " +
message);
    }
}
```

Usage

java

```java
Subject subject = new Subject();
Observer observer1 = new
ConcreteObserver("Observer 1");
```

```java
Observer observer2 = new
ConcreteObserver("Observer 2");


subject.addObserver(observer1);

subject.addObserver(observer2);


subject.notifyObservers("New Event");
// Output:
// Observer 1 received update: New Event
// Observer 2 received update: New Event
```

The Observer pattern allows multiple objects to listen for and respond to changes in another object's state.

Strategy Pattern

The **Strategy** pattern defines a family of algorithms, encapsulates each one, and makes them interchangeable. This allows the algorithm to vary independently from clients that use it.

Implementation Example

java

```java
interface PaymentStrategy {
    void pay(int amount);
```

```java
}


class CreditCardPayment implements PaymentStrategy
{
    public void pay(int amount) {
        System.out.println("Paid " + amount + " using
credit card.");
    }
}


class PayPalPayment implements PaymentStrategy {
    public void pay(int amount) {
        System.out.println("Paid " + amount + " using
PayPal.");
    }
}


class ShoppingCart {
    private PaymentStrategy paymentStrategy;


    public void setPaymentStrategy(PaymentStrategy
paymentStrategy) {
```

```java
        this.paymentStrategy = paymentStrategy;

    }


    public void checkout(int amount) {

        paymentStrategy.pay(amount);

    }
}
```

Usage

java


```java
ShoppingCart cart = new ShoppingCart();


cart.setPaymentStrategy(new CreditCardPayment());

cart.checkout(100); // Output: Paid 100 using credit card.


cart.setPaymentStrategy(new PayPalPayment());

cart.checkout(150); // Output: Paid 150 using PayPal.
```

The Strategy pattern allows switching between different payment methods dynamically.

14.4 Other Common Patterns in Java

While we've covered some key patterns, there are many others worth exploring. Here's a brief overview:

- **Builder Pattern**: Simplifies the construction of complex objects by providing a step-by-step approach.

- **Proxy Pattern**: Provides a surrogate for another object to control access to it, often used in lazy initialization or security scenarios.

- **Facade Pattern**: Simplifies complex subsystems by providing a unified interface, reducing dependencies between systems.

Each pattern has its own specific use cases, and the choice of pattern depends on the design requirements of the application.

14.5 Choosing the Right Pattern

Selecting the appropriate design pattern depends on the problem you're trying to solve. Consider the following:

1. **Identify Common Problems**: Recognize recurring design challenges in your code, such as complex object creation, tight coupling, or duplicated behavior.

2. **Analyze the Context**: Determine the flexibility, scalability, and maintainability requirements for the application.

3. **Start Simple**: Avoid overusing patterns; sometimes simpler solutions are better. Apply patterns only when they clearly improve the design.

Conclusion

Design patterns are essential tools for developing flexible, maintainable, and scalable Java applications. By understanding and applying patterns like Singleton, Factory, Adapter, Observer, and Strategy, you can solve common design problems, enhance code organization, and improve software quality. Design patterns provide a foundation for high-quality software design, allowing developers to leverage well-established solutions to complex problems.

In this chapter, we covered key creational, structural, and behavioral patterns, demonstrating how each can be applied in Java. Armed with this knowledge, you're now ready to design applications with the flexibility and structure necessary for real-world software development.

Chapter 15: Introduction to Spring Framework for Web Development

What is the Spring Framework?

The Spring Framework is an open-source, modular Java framework designed to make it easier to build Java applications by providing tools for dependency injection, data management, transaction handling, and web application support. Spring follows a modular architecture, allowing you to use only the components you need, making it suitable for everything from simple applications to complex enterprise systems.

Spring provides several key benefits:

- **Dependency Injection (DI)**: Simplifies object creation and dependency management, improving code flexibility.

- **Aspect-Oriented Programming (AOP)**: Enables modularizing cross-cutting concerns, such as logging and security.

- **Spring MVC**: A powerful framework for building web applications following the Model-View-Controller (MVC) pattern.

- **Spring Boot**: Simplifies configuration and setup, providing a quick way to create stand-alone applications with embedded servers.

15.1 Setting Up a Spring Project

Spring projects can be created easily using **Spring Initializr**, a web-based project generator that provides a base setup with Spring Boot.

Using Spring Initializr

1. **Go to Spring Initializr**: start.spring.io

2. **Configure Project**:

   o **Project**: Maven or Gradle

   o **Language**: Java

   o **Spring Boot Version**: Select the latest stable version.

- o **Project Metadata**: Set the Group (e.g., com.example) and Artifact (e.g., spring-demo).

3. **Select Dependencies**:

   - o **Spring Web**: Enables REST and MVC capabilities.

   - o **Spring Data JPA**: Provides data access support.

   - o **MySQL Driver** (or other database drivers): Allows database integration.

4. **Generate the Project**: Download the generated zip file, extract it, and open it in your IDE.

Spring Initializr provides a ready-to-run project structure, helping you get started with minimal setup.

15.2 Spring Core Concepts: Dependency Injection (DI) and Inversion of Control (IoC)

One of Spring's core principles is **Inversion of Control (IoC)**, where objects do not create their dependencies directly but instead receive them externally, known as **Dependency Injection (DI)**. DI decouples components, making code easier to test and maintain.

Example of Dependency Injection with Spring

Define a service class:

java

```java
import org.springframework.stereotype.Service;

@Service
public class GreetingService {
    public String greet() {
        return "Hello, Spring!";
    }
}
```

In the @Service annotated class, Spring manages the instantiation of GreetingService and makes it available to other components.

Now, inject this service into a controller class:

java

```java
import org.springframework.beans.factory.annotation.Autowired;
```

```java
import
org.springframework.web.bind.annotation.GetMappin
g;
import
org.springframework.web.bind.annotation.RestControl
ler;


@RestController
public class GreetingController {

    private final GreetingService greetingService;


    @Autowired
    public GreetingController(GreetingService
greetingService) {
        this.greetingService = greetingService;
    }


    @GetMapping("/greet")
    public String greet() {
        return greetingService.greet();
    }
```

```
}
```

In this example:

- The GreetingController is a REST controller that receives requests at the /greet endpoint.

- @Autowired injects the GreetingService dependency, decoupling the controller from the service's implementation details.

Spring manages the lifecycle of both components, instantiating GreetingService and injecting it wherever needed.

15.3 Introduction to Spring Boot

Spring Boot builds on top of the Spring Framework, simplifying application setup and configuration. With Spring Boot, you can create stand-alone applications that embed a web server (like Tomcat), removing the need for external deployment.

Benefits of Spring Boot

- **Auto-configuration**: Automatically configures components based on the dependencies in your project.

- **Embedded Web Server**: Allows applications to run independently without a separate web server.

- **Convention over Configuration**: Defaults to sensible configurations while allowing customizations as needed.

Running a Spring Boot Application

In the spring-demo project created with Spring Initializr, Spring Boot provides a main class annotated with @SpringBootApplication, which marks it as a bootstrapping class.

java

```java
import org.springframework.boot.SpringApplication;
import org.springframework.boot.autoconfigure.SpringBootApplication;

@SpringBootApplication
public class SpringDemoApplication {
    public static void main(String[] args) {

        SpringApplication.run(SpringDemoApplication.class, args);
    }
}
```

- **@SpringBootApplication**: Combines @Configuration, @EnableAutoConfiguration, and @ComponentScan, indicating that this is the main configuration class.

To start the application, run SpringDemoApplication from your IDE or by using the command:

bash

```
./mvnw spring-boot:run
```

Spring Boot starts an embedded Tomcat server on http://localhost:8080, where the application is accessible.

15.4 Building Web Applications with Spring MVC

Spring MVC (Model-View-Controller) is Spring's web framework for building web applications. It organizes code into three layers:

- **Model**: Manages application data.

- **View**: Represents the presentation layer.

- **Controller**: Handles user requests and determines the response.

Creating a REST Controller

A REST controller in Spring MVC provides endpoints to handle HTTP requests.

java

```java
import org.springframework.web.bind.annotation.GetMapping;
import org.springframework.web.bind.annotation.RequestParam;
import org.springframework.web.bind.annotation.RestController;

@RestController
public class CalculatorController {

    @GetMapping("/add")
    public String add(@RequestParam int a, @RequestParam int b) {
        int result = a + b;
        return "Result: " + result;
    }
}
```

}

This CalculatorController example:

- Defines an endpoint at /add that accepts two parameters (a and b).
- Uses @RequestParam to capture query parameters, adds the numbers, and returns the result as a string.

Handling HTTP POST Requests

To handle POST requests, use @PostMapping.

java

```java
import org.springframework.web.bind.annotation.*;

@RestController
public class MessageController {

    @PostMapping("/message")
    public String createMessage(@RequestBody String message) {
        return "Message received: " + message;
    }
}
```

In this example:

- @RequestBody binds the body of the HTTP request to a method parameter.

- @PostMapping allows the method to respond to POST requests at /message.

15.5 Accessing Data with Spring Data JPA

Spring Data JPA simplifies database access by providing an abstraction layer over JPA (Java Persistence API), reducing the need for boilerplate code. With Spring Data JPA, you can define repositories to manage entities with minimal configuration.

Setting Up Database Configuration

In application.properties, configure the database connection:

properties

spring.datasource.url=jdbc:mysql://localhost:3306/spring_demo

spring.datasource.username=root

spring.datasource.password=password

spring.jpa.hibernate.ddl-auto=update

Creating an Entity

Define an entity class representing a database table.

java

```java
import javax.persistence.Entity;
import javax.persistence.GeneratedValue;
import javax.persistence.GenerationType;
import javax.persistence.Id;

@Entity
public class Product {
    @Id
    @GeneratedValue(strategy = GenerationType.IDENTITY)
    private Long id;

    private String name;
    private double price;
```

```
// Getters and setters
```

}

- @Entity: Indicates that the Product class is a JPA entity.

- @Id and @GeneratedValue: Specify the primary key and auto-generation strategy.

Creating a Repository

The repository interface provides data access methods without writing SQL or database code.

java

```
import org.springframework.data.jpa.repository.JpaRepository;


public interface ProductRepository extends JpaRepository<Product, Long> {

}
```

ProductRepository extends JpaRepository, which provides CRUD operations for the Product entity.

Using the Repository in a Service

Inject the repository into a service class to handle business logic.

```java

import org.springframework.beans.factory.annotation.Autowired;
import org.springframework.stereotype.Service;

import java.util.List;

@Service
public class ProductService {

    @Autowired
    private ProductRepository productRepository;

    public List<Product> getAllProducts() {
        return productRepository.findAll();
    }

    public Product saveProduct(Product product) {
        return productRepository.save(product);
```

```
    }
}
```

With ProductService, you can access and manage products without writing SQL code.

15.6 Building a Simple REST API

Now let's bring everything together by building a REST API for managing products.

Product Controller

java

```java
import org.springframework.beans.factory.annotation.Autowired;

import org.springframework.web.bind.annotation.*;

import java.util.List;

@RestController
@RequestMapping("/api/products")
public class ProductController {
```

```
@Autowired

private ProductService productService;


@GetMapping

public List<Product> getAllProducts() {

    return productService.getAllProducts();

}


@PostMapping

public Product createProduct(@RequestBody
Product product) {

    return productService.saveProduct(product);

}

}
```

In this example:

- @RequestMapping("/api/products") defines a base URL for all product-related endpoints.

- @GetMapping returns a list of all products.

- @PostMapping creates a new product with data provided in the request body.

Testing the API

To test the API, use a tool like **Postman** or **curl**.

- **GET Request**: Retrieve all products.

bash

```
curl -X GET http://localhost:8080/api/products
```

- **POST Request**: Add a new product.

bash

```
curl -X POST http://localhost:8080/api/products -H
"Content-Type: application/json" -d '{"name":
"Laptop", "price": 899.99}'
```

This simple API demonstrates the core of a Spring-based REST application.

15.7 Spring Security (Optional)

Spring Security provides authentication and authorization features to secure applications. Adding Spring Security to the project requires including the spring-boot-starter-security dependency, which enforces basic authentication by default.

To configure Spring Security:

1. Add the dependency in pom.xml.

2. Create a SecurityConfig class with custom security settings.

For instance, the following example disables CSRF and allows public access to /api/products:

java

```java
import org.springframework.context.annotation.Configuration;
import org.springframework.security.config.annotation.web.builders.HttpSecurity;
import org.springframework.security.config.annotation.web.configuration.WebSecurityConfigurerAdapter;

@Configuration
public class SecurityConfig extends WebSecurityConfigurerAdapter {

    @Override
    protected void configure(HttpSecurity http) throws Exception {
        http.csrf().disable()
```

```
.authorizeRequests()

.antMatchers("/api/products").permitAll()

.anyRequest().authenticated();

    }

}
```

Spring Security can handle everything from basic authentication to OAuth2, enabling secure applications.

15.8 Deploying a Spring Boot Application

You can deploy Spring Boot applications easily by packaging them as JAR files with embedded servers.

1. **Package the Application**:

Use Maven to package the application as a JAR:

bash

```
mvn clean package
```

This creates an executable JAR file in the target directory.

2. **Run the JAR**:

Start the application using:

bash

```
java -jar target/spring-demo-0.0.1-SNAPSHOT.jar
```

Spring Boot applications can also be deployed to platforms like AWS, Heroku, or Google Cloud for broader accessibility.

Conclusion

In this chapter, you learned the basics of the Spring Framework for web development, focusing on dependency injection, Spring Boot, Spring MVC, and Spring Data JPA. You built a simple REST API, managed data with Spring Data JPA, and explored how Spring Boot automates configuration and setup, simplifying the development process. With these foundations, you can confidently start building more complex Java web applications using the Spring Framework.

In the next chapter, we'll explore advanced Spring concepts like Spring Security, Spring REST, and more, to further enhance your understanding of the Spring ecosystem for professional-grade applications.

Conclusion: Mastering Java for Real-World Development

As we reach the conclusion of "The Complete Java Developer's Handbook," you've journeyed through the expansive landscape of Java, from mastering the syntax and fundamentals to building full-scale, professional applications. Along the way, you've delved into advanced topics that equip you with the skills to tackle real-world software development challenges. This book aimed to not only make you proficient in Java as a programming language but also empower you to design, develop, and deploy robust applications that adhere to industry standards.

Let's take a moment to recap and appreciate the skills and knowledge you've gained, and discuss how you can continue growing as a Java developer.

From Syntax to Sophisticated Systems

Starting from the basics, you familiarized yourself with Java's core syntax, object-oriented programming principles, and foundational structures. This foundation is indispensable, as it allows you to understand not only how Java programs work but also why they work. Concepts like data types, control structures, and exception handling formed the backbone of your journey, preparing you to write code that is both efficient and resilient.

From there, you built upon your knowledge with a deep dive into **Object-Oriented Programming (OOP)**—one of Java's most defining features. By mastering encapsulation, inheritance, polymorphism, and abstraction, you learned how to create modular, reusable, and maintainable code. Understanding these principles equips you with the skills to model real-world problems in code, a skill essential in professional software development.

Through this book's step-by-step approach, you also explored **data management** with collections, **error handling** with exceptions, and the intricacies of **Java's Input/Output (I/O) system**. These essential building blocks allow you to process data reliably, handle unexpected conditions gracefully, and ensure that your applications interact with the external world seamlessly.

Harnessing Concurrency and Networking

In today's fast-paced technological world, applications that can perform multiple tasks simultaneously are highly valued. This book dedicated a comprehensive section to **multithreading and concurrency** in Java, demystifying complex topics like thread management, synchronization, and inter-thread communication. With these skills, you're now capable of building responsive applications that can handle intensive workloads without compromising on performance.

Networking capabilities further extended your knowledge, allowing your applications to communicate with other systems over the internet. You learned how to connect to servers, handle URLs, and use the HttpURLConnection class to fetch data. You also built practical networking projects, such as a simple file transfer system and an API client, demonstrating how Java's networking features make it possible to create web-enabled applications.

Building Dynamic and Interactive Applications with JavaFX and JDBC

In the modern software landscape, user interaction is key, and JavaFX brought that to life in this book. By working through examples, you explored how to create **Graphical User Interfaces (GUIs)**, manage layouts, handle events, and make applications that are both dynamic and visually engaging. JavaFX's powerful features, combined with your knowledge of Java, open up endless possibilities for creating professional-grade desktop applications.

To make applications that can persist data, you also learned to work with **databases** through **JDBC**. Managing data effectively is crucial in real-world applications, and with JDBC, you now have the tools to connect your applications to a database, manage data with SQL commands, and apply best practices like transactions and connection pooling. These skills enable you to build data-driven applications that can scale with growing user demands.

Real-World Project Integration

Learning isolated concepts is one thing, but integrating them into cohesive projects is where the real power of programming lies. This book's **final project** brought together everything you've learned, from building an intuitive UI to managing data with JDBC and handling background tasks with multithreading. Projects like these demonstrate how to transform concepts into working applications, preparing you for the types of challenges faced in professional development.

This capstone experience not only consolidated your skills but also gave you insights into the structure, organization, and discipline required in software engineering. This kind of hands-on learning is essential, as it bridges the gap between theory and practice, allowing you to transition smoothly from a student of Java to a proficient developer.

Ensuring Quality and Reliability with Testing and Design Patterns

Building reliable software goes beyond writing code that works; it involves creating code that can stand the test of time. This book dedicated chapters to **unit testing with JUnit** and **Test-Driven Development (TDD)**, teaching you to think critically about your code from a quality perspective. Writing tests ensures that your code behaves as expected and remains stable as you expand your applications. Embracing TDD encourages a mindset where testing becomes an integral part of development, ensuring your applications are both robust and resilient.

Design patterns further enhanced your knowledge by teaching you how to solve common problems with established, best-practice solutions. Patterns like Singleton, Factory, Observer, and Strategy help you design software that is modular, extensible, and maintainable. These patterns are indispensable tools for developers, as they provide a shared vocabulary and guide software design across projects and teams.

Exploring the Power of the Spring Framework

The **Spring Framework** has transformed Java into one of the most powerful platforms for web development, and in this book, you got a taste of its capabilities. By learning the fundamentals of Spring, you're now able to create efficient and scalable web applications. Spring Boot made it possible to rapidly develop standalone applications with minimal configuration, while Spring MVC and Spring Data JPA empowered you to create REST APIs and manage data effortlessly.

Spring's principles of dependency injection and inversion of control promote clean, modular code that is easy to test and maintain. As you explore Spring further, you'll find that its ecosystem extends into areas like security, messaging, and cloud-native development, equipping you with tools to tackle large-scale applications.

Beyond This Book: Advancing Your Java Career

This book has given you a comprehensive foundation in Java, but learning never stops in the world of technology. Here are some paths you might consider as you continue your journey:

1. **Deepen Your Knowledge of Advanced Java**: Topics like **reflection, annotations**, and **Java bytecode manipulation** are advanced concepts that allow you to write highly flexible, efficient code.

2. **Mastering Enterprise Java**: Dive deeper into the **Spring ecosystem**, exploring modules like Spring Security for application security, Spring Cloud for microservices architecture, and Spring Batch for handling large-scale batch processing.

3. **Explore Other JVM Languages**: Learning languages like **Kotlin** and **Scala**, which run on the Java Virtual Machine (JVM), can broaden your understanding of functional programming, conciseness, and other advanced paradigms.

4. **Specialize in Big Data and Machine Learning**: Libraries like **Apache Spark** and **Hadoop** make Java an excellent choice for big data processing. Additionally, frameworks like **DL4J** (Deep Learning for Java) bring machine learning capabilities to the Java ecosystem.

5. **Develop Your DevOps Skills**: With tools like **Docker**, **Kubernetes**, and **CI/CD** pipelines, you can become proficient in deploying and scaling Java applications on cloud platforms like AWS, Azure, or Google Cloud.

Final Words: Embrace Continuous Learning and Growth

Java has been one of the most enduring languages in software development due to its performance, scalability, and adaptability. The skills you've gained here, including the understanding of OOP, multithreading, web development, data handling, testing, and design patterns, are highly transferable and foundational to other areas in software engineering. The discipline of TDD, the power of design patterns, and the knowledge of frameworks like Spring are invaluable assets in any developer's toolkit.

As you advance, remember that the best developers are those who continuously learn and adapt. The software development field is ever-evolving, with new frameworks, tools, and paradigms constantly emerging. Keep exploring, building projects, and collaborating with other developers. Each project you undertake will not only hone your skills but also deepen your understanding of what it means to create impactful, reliable, and efficient software.

Congratulations on completing "The Complete Java Developer's Handbook"! You are now well-equipped to make meaningful contributions in the world of Java development and beyond. Embrace the journey ahead with confidence, curiosity, and the knowledge that you have a strong foundation to support you every step of the way. Whether you build your own applications, contribute to open source projects, or work with teams in enterprise settings, you now have the skills and mindset to tackle real-world problems and create software that makes a difference.

Happy coding, and welcome to the world of professional Java development!